Increasing Formality and Productivity of Bolivian Firms

THE WORLD BANK
Washington, D.C.

ISBN-13: 978-0-8213-8023-9
eISBN: 978-0-8213-8024-6
ISSN: 0253-2123   DOI: 10.1596/978-0-8213-8023-9

Library of Congress Cataloging-in-Publication Data has been requested.

Contents

Tables

Figures

Boxes

Preface

Bolivia's informal sector is the largest in Latin America, by many definitions and measures. Bolivia's high informality rate has been blamed on many factors including the burden of regulation, the weakness of public institutions, and the lack of perceived benefits to being formal. The high level of informality has a number of negative implications for low productivity, low growth, and low quality of jobs.

This study presents the results of a study conducted at the request of the Bolivian authorities on informality. The study undertakes fresh qualitative and quantitative analyses to better understand the reasons why firms are informal and the impact of formalization on their profitability, in order to inform policy actions appropriate to the reality of Bolivia.

The results of the analysis indicate that formality follows a continuum, starting with municipal licenses, then getting a tax number, and finally signing up with the national firm registry. Lack of information on formality is a major determinant of firms' decision to remain informal. Lack of perceived benefits of formality is the other most important reason.

The crucial finding of the analysis is that the impact of tax registration on profitability depends on firm size and the ability to issue tax receipts. The smallest and the largest firms in the sample have lower profits as a result of tax registration because their cost of formalizing exceeds benefits. Firms in the middle range (two to five employees) benefit from tax registration in large part due to increasing the customer base by issuing tax receipts. The analysis also shows that decisions about formality depend on the entrepreneur's self-efficacy—measuring his ability and confidence to run a business—the entrepreneur's reason for entering into business, and the level of enforcement.

Based on the quantitative and qualitative analysis, the book presents a set of prioritized policy implications. In the short term, the priority should be to increase the benefits of formalization through training, access to credit and markets, and other forms of business support. The second priority in the short term with low cost and high potential impact is to increase information on how to formalize and its benefits. In the medium term, the priority is to simplify formalization, regulatory and taxation procedures, and reduce their costs. Increasing even-handed enforcement of taxation and regulation is also important to promote formality, although it should not be the priority for micro and small firms. Measures to boost the productivity of micro and small firms in general will help overall economic growth, employment, and formalization.

Abstract

Bolivia's informal sector is the largest in Latin America, by many definitions and measures. Bolivia's high informality rate has been blamed on many factors including the burden of regulation, the weakness of public institutions, and the lack of perceived benefits to being formal. The high level of informality has a number of negative implications related to for low productivity, low growth, and low quality of jobs.

This study presents fresh qualitative and quantitative analyses to better understand the reasons why firms are informal and the impact of formalization on their profitability, in order to inform policy actions appropriate to the reality of Bolivia.

The crucial finding of the analysis is that the impact of tax registration on profitability depends on firm size and the ability to issue tax receipts. The smallest and the largest firms in the sample have lower profits as a result of tax registration because their cost of formalizing exceeds benefits. Firms in the middle range (two to five employees) benefit from tax registration in large part due to increasing the customer base by issuing tax receipts.

The study presents a set of prioritized policy implications for policy makers. In the short term, the first priority should be to increase the benefits of formalization through training, access to credit and markets, and business support. The second priority is to increase information on how to formalize and its benefits. In the medium term, the priority is to simplify formalization, regulatory, and taxation procedures and to reduce their costs. Increasing even-handed enforcement of taxation and regulation is also important but not a priority for micro and small firms. Measures to boost the productivity of micro and small firms in general will help overall economic growth, employment, and formalization.

Acknowledgments

This report was prepared by a team led by Yaye Seynabou Sakho (LCSPE) and comprising David McKenzie (DECRG), Julio Loayza (LCCBO), and Julio Velasco (LCCBO). The peer reviewers for this report are Bill Maloney (Lead Economist LCRCE), Vincent Palmade (Lead Economist FIAS-IFC), and Wilson Jimenez (UNDP-Bolivia).

The report was prepared under the guidance and supervision of Mauricio Carrizosa (Sector Manager LCSPE) and Vicente Fretes Cibils (Lead Economist and PREM Sector Leader LCSPE). Marcelo Giugale (Country Director, LCC6A) linked the team to the Bank's overall strategy and steered them in that direction.

The report benefited from excellent contributions from Fernando Landa and Jose Ramirez (UDAPE), Pablo Fajnzylber (LCSFP), Chris Humphrey (LCC6A), Michael Geller (LCSPE), Jean Clevy (LCSPE), and Carol Rosen. The gender components throughout this report were based on contributions from Maria Dolores Arriba Banos (LCC6A), Trine Lunde (LCSPP), Lykke Andersen (INESAD, Bolivia), Beatriz Muriel (INESAD, Bolivia), and Ruth Llanos (LCSSO). Financial support provided by the Gender Action Plan (GAP) for the preparation of the gender contribution to the report is gratefully acknowledged.

This report was enhanced by substantive comments from a variety of people during various stages of this project. Comments were received from: Dena Ringold (LCSHD), Ian Walker (LCSHS), Chris Humphrey (LCC6A), Tom Kenyon (FIAS-IFC), Fernando Landa (UDAPE, Bolivia), Carlos Mollinedo and Jaime Ortega (IFC Bolivia), Mike Goldberg (LCFPD), Wendy Cunningham (LSCHS), Marcos Kucharsky (Vice Minister of Planning and Coordination, Bolivia), and Syed Mahmood (SASFP).

The report was prepared based on two missions in Bolivia that took place in October 2006 and February 2007. The team would like to thank the Bolivian authorities, including UDAPE, INE, Ministry of Planning through VIPFE, and the Vice Ministry of Planning and Coordination for their cooperation in delineating the scope of the study and facilitating access to all the information necessary for the study. In particular, Noel Aguirre (Vice Ministry of Planning and Coordination), who coordinated an inter-ministerial working group to provide input for the study *Encuestas & Estudios*, is acknowledged for collecting the qualitative and quantitative data.

The team gratefully acknowledges all the support received.

Abbreviations and Acronyms

AFP	*Administradoras de Fondos de Pensiones* (Pension Funds Administrators)
ASOFIN	*Asociación de Entidades Financieras Especializadas en Micro Finanzas de Bolivia* (Association of Bolivian Financial Entities Specializing in Micro-Finance)
BCB	*Banco Central de Bolivia* (Central Bank of Bolivia)
CEPROBOL	*Centro de Promoción Bolivia*
CEPB	*Confederación de Empresarios Privados de Bolivia* (Confederation of Bolivian Private Businessmen)
CG	Consultative Group
DFID	Department for International Development (UK)
FONDESIF	*Fondo de Desarrollo del Sistema Financiero y de Apoyo al Sector Productivo* (Fund for the Development of the Financial Sector and for Support to the Productive Sector)
GDP	Gross domestic product
IDA	International Development Association
IDB	Inter-American Development Bank
ILO	International Labor Organization
IMF	International Monetary Fund
INE	*Instituto Nacional de Estadísticas* (National Statistics Institute)
INESAD	Institute for Advanced Development Studies
MAS	*Movimiento al Socialismo* (Movement to Socialism)
MDGs	Millennium Development Goals
MDRI	Multilateral Debt Relief Initiative
MECOVI	*Encuesta de Mejoramiento de Condiciones de Vida* (Survey on Improvement in Living Conditions)
MEFs	Microfinance Entities
NAFIBO	*Nacional Financiera Boliviana* (Bolivian National Financial Fund)
NGO	Nongovernmental organization
NIT	Tax identification number
OECD	Organization for Economic Cooperation and Development
PFFs	Private Financial Funds
PRSP	Poverty Reduction Strategy Paper
SBEF	*Superintendencia de Bancos y Entidades Financieras* (Superintendency of Banks and Financial Entities of Bolivia)

Republic of Bolivia Fiscal Year
January 1 to December 31

Currency Equivalents
(as of September 28, 2006)
Currency Unit = Bolivianos
1 US Dollar = Bs. 8.00

Weights and Measures
Metric System

Vice President, LCR:	Pamela Cox
Director, LCC6C:	Marcelo Giugale
Director, LCSPR:	Ernesto May
Sector Manager, LCSPE:	Mauricio Carrizosa
Sector Leader, LCSPE:	Vicente Fretes Cibils
Task Team Leader:	Yaye Seynabou Sakho

Executive Summary

Overview of Informality

Bolivia's informal sector is the largest in Latin America, by many definitions and measures. Nearly 80 percent of urban and rural employment in Bolivia is informal, which is the highest level in Latin America. The average share of informal employment across the region is below 60 percent. Bolivia leads the world in value-added generated by the informal sector as a share of gross domestic product, estimated at 68 percent. Informality in Bolivia is also the highest in the region under a legalistic definition based on the right to a retirement pension linked to employment. About 70 percent of workers are not registered in the pension system—the highest in the region, along with Paraguay.

Bolivia's high informality rate has been blamed on many factors including the burden of regulation, the weakness of public institutions, and the lack of perceived benefits to being formal. The regulatory complexity affecting formal firms has been blamed as one of the main causes of informality. For example, registry requirements to create a firm are very expensive—up to 140 percent of the average annual income. In addition, the regulatory regime is so restrictive that Bolivia ranks 113 out of 175 countries included in the *Doing Business 2007* report, above only Haiti and República Bolivariana de Venezuela in Latin America. However, the much higher rate of informality in Bolivia compared to other countries in the region with similar regulatory burdens suggests that other issues are also involved, including those related to quality of public institutions. Weak public institutions magnify the burden of regulation. Hence, the government's capacity to apply the law is lowered, reducing the risk of penalties for informal firms, as well as the capacity of public agencies to simplify regulation without creating legal loopholes. Complex regulations enacted by governments that lack the capability to enforce compliance encourage informality. These problems are compounded by the lack and high cost of information on what a business needs to do to become and remain formal. Finally, there is a wide perception that the benefits of becoming formal are largely offset by the costs associated among others with the regulatory burden.

This high level of informality has a number of negative implications for Bolivia related to economic growth, the financing of public goods, and the integrity of public and private institutions. Informal firms tend to have low productivity because they have limited access to physical, financial, and human capital to produce more efficiently and grow. Some informal firms maintain a low scale of operations to avoid being visible to enforcement. The small scale of informal operations traps labor and resources in low-productivity activities, which limits the economies overall potential for economic growth. There are also negative fiscal implications from high informality: although informal firms generate government revenue through some unavoidable taxes such as value-added taxes, they do not pay income and other taxes or fees for some government services, and as a result are "free riders" on public services that are provided with fiscal resources. And on a broader level, the fact that so much of the economy is technically illegal undermines respect for the rule of law and public institutions, encourages corruption, and weakens the enforceability of contracts, all of which limit Bolivia's ability to develop economically, politically, and socially. While informality is a rational decision and one could argue that the market should resolve the issue by itself, the many important negative social externalities that result argue for public policy to improve this situation.

Productivity and Profitability of Informal Firms

This study undertook fresh qualitative and quantitative analyses to gain a better understanding of the reasons firms chose to be informal or not, and the impact of formalization on the productivity and profitability of informal firms, to inform policy recommendations appropriate to the reality of Bolivia's informal sector. The study draws upon a thorough qualitative analysis based on focus group interviews with formal and informal firms in La Paz, El Alto, Cochabamba, and Santa Cruz, as well as a new quantitative survey of firms in six industries. The qualitative analysis allows the identification of the main sector-specific and general constraints to formalization and to higher productivity. The quantitative micro study, based on a specialized survey of more than 600 micro, small, and medium enterprises, both formal and informal, provides credible empirical evidence on the determinants of formality at the firm level and the effects of informality on the profitability of a variety of firms. These findings shed new light on the determinants of a firm's decision to become formal, the consequences of this decision for profits depending on the size of the firm, and some of the potential channels through which profits are affected. While many of the results regarding productivity and profitability are applicable to firms in different places on the continuum of formality, the extremely high degree of informality among all micro and small firms means that conclusions are highly relevant to addressing the situation of informal firms in Bolivia.

Survey results indicate that formality follows a continuum, starting with municipal licenses, then getting a tax number, and finally signing up with the national firm registry. Of the 630 firms surveyed—which are census representative at the urban level—just under half were completely informal, 28 percent only had a municipal license, 21 percent had a tax number and a municipal license, and only 4 percent had a license, tax number, and were in the national firm registry. Formalization is particularly low in rural areas, with 10 percent of rural companies having a tax number and none in the national firm registry, suggesting both the impact of higher travel time to formalize and also weaker enforcement in rural areas.

Lack of information on formality is a major determinant of firms' decision to remain informal. Many informal firms do not know how, where, and why to become formal. Few firms have knowledge of the steps to register a business, obtain a tax number and file regular tax declarations, or conform to complex labor regulations. There is also a lack of knowledge about the role and functions of the national registry FundEmpresa. Over 40 percent of firms registered there do not know its role or what benefits it provides. Micro and small firms ignore how paying taxes is used for the provision of public services that will benefit them.

Lack of perceived benefits of formality is the other most important reason for micro and small firms to remain informal. For informal micro and small firms the perceived benefits from formalizing were far outweighed by the high costs in terms of tax and labor payments and of dealing with a complex and inefficient bureaucracy. Many firms report that the costs of formalization are not offset by any benefits giving them few incentives to comply with the procedures to become formal, except in the case of exporting firms. For formal firms the main benefits of formalizing were to obey the law and avoid fines.

Among entrepreneurs in micro and small firms, decisions about formality depend on the entrepreneur's self-efficacy (the ability and confidence to run a business), the entrepreneur's reasons for entering into business, and the level of enforcement. Among micro and small firms in the quantitative survey, the more able entrepreneurs are formal. Entrepreneurs who went into business to make profits and expand their firm also tend to favor formality, while those who started informal businesses to have more flexibility to take care of family responsibilities usually keep their firms informal. Larger informal firms tend to be operated by more able entrepreneurs, who see little benefit in formalizing.

The survey indicates that the impact of formality on profitability depends on the size of the firm and its ability to issue formal receipts. Both a municipal license and a tax number are associated with increased profits for the average firm formalizing. However, the smallest and the largest firms in the sample see lower profits as a result of becoming formal, because their cost of regulation exceeds benefits. The increase in profits from having a tax number appears in large part due to increasing the customer base related to the issuing of receipts. It does not come from higher mark-ups, lower input prices, or better access to credit. Firms with a tax number also view corruption as less of an obstacle, suggesting a reduction in bribes. However, they pay more taxes and are more likely to view labor laws as constraints to further business growth.

Female entrepreneurs have higher level of informality and earn lower profits than male entrepreneurs. However, these differences can be explained by the reasons why they decide to enter into self-employment (for example, to take care of family), their lower education and self ability, the sectors they choose to work, and finally the smaller scale of their operation compared to male entrepreneurs.

The impact of formality on the functioning of firms assessed from the qualitative analysis based on focus groups interviews suggests that small firms reap more benefits from operating formally than micro firms. Informality shields informal micro firms from the costs of doing business related to formality such as costly customs, labor, and trade regulation, and taxes. In contrast, formality does not provide any significant benefits to micro firms. However, as firm size increases from micro to small, formality is associated with more benefits including easier access to credit and equipment and less exposure to corruption.

The qualitative analysis based on focus groups reveals that access to capital seems to be the main constraint to productivity for all micro and small firms. However, the survey indicates that while registering at the municipal level improves firms' access to finance, getting a tax number does not. Micro and small firms have access to a narrower set of financing mechanisms and at a higher cost. Informality slightly exacerbates the access to credit issue that micro and small firms face. This reduced access forces micro and small firms to rely more heavily on savings and resources lent by family and friends. As a result, micro and small firms have greater difficulty obtaining better equipment, technology, higher-quality inputs, and other factors needed to expand their business.. However, the quantitative analysis suggests that becoming formal only increases access to finance for firms registered at the municipal level, in contrast getting a tax number does not.

Overall, functioning and profitability of micro and small firms are affected by many variables in addition to whether firms operate formally or informally. Both focus groups and survey results indicate that key micro constraints to productivity include limited access to financial services and skilled labor, quality inputs, and technology. On the macro side, significant operational constraints to increased productivity include macroeconomic and political instability, inadequate public infrastructure, corruption, and crime.

Policy Recommendations

In the short term, the priority should be efforts to increase the benefits of formalization through training, access to credit and markets, and other forms of business support. Formality could be made more attractive by improving the provision of business development and training services available to formal firms, and by facilitating access to product markets through public procurement opportunities, developing the domestic market with products of better quality and price, export promotion programs, and supplier development programs aimed at increasing linkages with larger private firms. Other ways of making formality more attractive include linking formalization with access to credit and improving the quality of legal services available to small businesses, so that they may find it less risky to expand beyond local markets.

The second priority in the short term with low cost and high potential impact on formalization is to increase information on how to formalize and its benefits. Both the focus groups and the survey clearly show that many informal businesses simply lack the necessary information on how to become and remain formal and do not perceive that there are any benefits to formalizing. Public actions to improve information about the different steps to formalization, promoting what firms can gain by becoming formal and what they risk by staying informal, have the potential to increase awareness and build the first step toward formalization. The dissemination of the information could be done through information centers and advisory services, radio broadcasts, and newsletters about locations to obtain information on formalization. Simplifying registration and tax procedures (discussed below) will also go a long way to reducing the cost of getting the necessary information on formality.

In the medium term, the priority is to simplify formalization, regulatory and taxation procedures and reduce their costs. Simplification measures have had some limited positive impact on increasing registration of micro firms in Brazil and Mexico, and at the municipal level in Bolivia. However, the impact of administrative simplification programs may be larger when accompanied by other complementary measures aimed, first, at increasing the potential benefits of joining the formal sector—e.g., facilitating access to credit or government provided technical assistance—or, second, at reducing other costs of regulatory compliance, beyond the facilitation of firm registration. The challenge is to distinguish relevant from anachronistic regulations and balance private costs from legitimate public interests, such as the protection of public safety or the environment. Improving the simplified tax regime for micro and small enterprises is also an essential component to provide incentives for formalization—considering that so few micro and small companies now pay any business taxes. The survey results further suggest that having a tax number increases profitability through the ability of issuing tax-deductible receipts to customers. Hence, making the tax regime attractive to small firms would prove to be a net gain for both the fiscal accounts and for formalization.

Increasing even-handed enforcement of taxation and regulations is also important to promote formality, although it should not be the top priority at this time for micro and small firms. The study provides evidence in support of the thesis that enforcement costs are strong determinants of the decision to get a tax number. Firms in industries and cities with high inspection rates are more likely to register, while those who operate their business further away from the tax offices are less likely. Enforcement should hence be increased further from the urban areas and the location far from tax offices. However, policies to reduce informality through stronger enforcement should be considered secondary to more positive incentives at this point, and should be implemented gradually and with significant previous publicity. The objective is not to capture businesspeople disobeying the law, but to encourage businesspeople to obey the law.

Measures to boost the productivity of micro and small firms in general will both help overall economic growth, employment, and, indirectly, formalization. Improving asset registration, streamlining collateral procedures, increasing the coverage of credit bureaus, and helping small firms improve their financial statements and supporting financial records can help with the critical productivity constraint of difficult access to credit by micro and small firms. Broader measures to facilitate technology adoption by domestic companies, improving public education to develop a better-prepared workforce, maintaining macroeconomic and political stability, and reducing corruption will all also help strengthen the productivity of firms, which in turn will tend toward greater formalization.

INTRODUCTION

Increasing Formality and Productivity of Bolivian Firms

Bolivia has experienced persistently high rate of informality and low average economic growth in the last decades. Nearly 80 percent of the active population, in rural and urban areas, is employed in the informal sector as a mix of workers, including new entrants, the disadvantaged and unemployed, and successful entrepreneurs. They have all sought alternatives to the strictures of formal employment. In the 1990s, Bolivia implemented ambitious economic reforms, including privatizations, liberalization of the exchange and trade systems, and revision of the pension systems. Those efforts have yielded a more resilient policy and financial environment, as well as more favorable social indicators. Nonetheless, economic growth, which has been driven mostly by extractive industries, has not been sustained, averaging only 0.3 percent over 1970–2005. As a consequence, 61 percent of the population remains in poverty, and income inequality is still very high, with a Gini coefficient of around 0.6 in 2005.

What Lies Behind Bolivia's Large Informal Sector?

The size of the informal sector has been blamed on many factors. The heavy regulation of formal firms and the weak climate for investment are reasons frequently given for the high rate of informality in Bolivia. Bolivia's business environment ranks 113 out of 175 countries included in the *Doing Business 2007* report (World Bank and IFC 2006), only above Haiti and República Bolivariana de Venezuela in Latin America. Informality is also seen as another symptom of public failure to provide basic public services, protection, and opportunities, pushing people to work in a state-free environment (World Bank 2007). A related hypothesis suggests that the size of the informal sector in Bolivia is due to the high costs of becoming formal versus the small benefits.

The size of the informal sector in the Bolivian economy has negative implications for economic growth and the provision of public services. One would expect that informality would be inversely related to the level of development of a country. However, there is limited empirical evidence linking the rate of self-employment and growth[1]. Yet, gains in productivity for micro, small, and medium firms have the potential to generate more output and to ripple through the economy as incomes and GDP grow. Higher growth would also imply less poverty, more jobs, and better opportunities to improve education and health.

The informal sector is characterized by low productivity with negative implications for total factor productivity growth. Informal micro enterprises reportedly generate 83 percent of the total employment, but only 25 percent of GDP (UDAPE 2003). In the manufacturing sector, 72 percent of employment is informal, but those workers produce only 20 percent of the aggregated value of the manufacturing sector (Larrazabal 1997). The tepid growth of total factor productivity, at 0.2 percent over 1970–2000, is one of the lowest in the world (Loayza 2004).

The production of small and informal firms is constrained by low access to credit, despite the evidence that returns to capital are highest for the smallest firms. Small firms and informal firms have more difficulty accessing productive inputs than larger firms, as it is very costly and risky to provide credit to small firms as compared to larger firms. As a consequence, many small firms are operating below their efficient scale of production.

Higher productivity is associated with higher formality. A large informal sector—which draws firms with less capital and workers with less education than in the formal sector—can result in a low level of productivity for the economy as a whole. Informal firms can trap labor and otherwise productive resources into low-productivity activities by maintaining a small scale of operation. In contrast, formal firms, often operating on a larger scale and enjoying better access to credit and to markets, are able to use capital, labor, and physical inputs more productively and raise economic productivity overall.

The current National Development Plan—*Plan Nacional de Desarrollo* (PND)—is focused on the productive development of micro and small firms and on the provision of incentives for firms to formalize. The PND addresses the issue through a three-pronged approach. First, the PND proposes the creation of a second tier Development Bank that would improve access to finance to rural producers and urban micro and small firms to increase their capacity and productivity. Second, the PND develops a policy of productive inclusion which provides incentives to the re-organization of production through vertical and horizontal integration of productive clusters (Complejos Productivos). Finally, the PND argues for the provision of subsidies to formalize enterprises and to promote quality certification and markets promotion.

How Does this Study Address the Problem?

Against the background of the PND, the study provides policy recommendations to increase the productivity of micro and small firms and to provide incentives for firms to formalize based on a fresh understanding of firms' behavior regarding formality, productivity, and profitability. The study investigates the determinants of firms' decision to formalize from sectoral, qualitative, and quantitative perspectives. It quantifies the impact of formality on the profitability of micro and small firms. It also investigates the channels through which formality affects firms' profitability. Based on these analyses, the study formulates policy recommendations, customized to suit the size and other characteristics of informal micro and small firms in Bolivia today. Those recommendations can increase formalization, raise productivity, and generate income and growth.

The study draws upon a fresh qualitative analysis based on focus group interviews and a new quantitative survey of firms in six industries. The qualitative analysis allows us to identify the main sector-specific and general constraints to formalization and to higher productivity for micro and small firms. The quantitative micro study, based on a specialized survey of more than 600 micro, small, and medium enterprises, provides empirical evidence on the determinants of formality at the firm level and the effects of formality on the profitability of a variety of firms. Our findings shed light on the determinants of a firm's decision to become formal, the consequences of this decision for profits, and some of the potential channels through which profits are affected. In particular, the study identifies the effects of physical, financial, and human capital and of the operational, institutional, and regulatory environment on profitability. Box 1 presents the study's methodology and main finding related to the causality between informality and firm profitability and evidence on the impact of formality on firm's profitability as a function of firm size.

Box 1. Are informal firms less profitable, or are less profitable firms just more likely to remain informal?

While there are theoretical reasons to think that informality may cause less growth for the country as a whole, there is little empirical evidence to support it. Economic theory would also suggest that a rational firm would only choose to stay informal if doing so is more profitable than becoming formal. As a result, less productive, smaller firms, who stand to gain less from the benefits of formality, will remain informal—so that low productivity causes informality rather than vice versa. This possible reverse causality has meant that previous research has not been able to conclusively show that informality causes lower profitability.

This study (chapter 3) provides new evidence which shows a direct and causal link from informality to lower profits *for some firms*—for other firms we find becoming formal actually lowers profits. Our new survey data and qualitative research show that many firms are simply unaware of the procedures for becoming formal. As a result, there are firms for which it would be profitable to become formal, who do not do so due to lack of information. Our instrumental variables estimation uses the GPS-measured distance from a firm to the office where registration for a tax identification number occurs as an instrumental variable for formality. We argue that, conditional on distance to the city center, how close a firm is to the tax office should affect its knowledge and cost of getting a tax identification number, but should not independently affect its profitability. This allows us to compute the effect of becoming formal for firms for which lack of information is the prime reason for staying informal. For such firms, we find that getting a tax identification number leads to large increases in profits, primarily by allowing them to expand their customer base.

We also use a technique called propensity score matching to compare firms which are similar in all observable characteristics apart from their registration status. Doing this reveals that micro and medium firms have lower profits after becoming formal, whereas small (two to five workers) firms see increases in profits from obtaining a municipal license or tax identification number.

Overall this analysis supports the view that many firms are making rational choices about whether or not to become formal under the current system, but it also shows that a lack of information about registration and a lack of benefits related to formalization prevent many of them from choosing to become formal.

The study is organized as follows:

- The first chapter of the report examines the different aspects of informality in Bolivia today. In particular, it discusses the size of the informal sector based on different definitions and measures. The chapter then describes who is in the informal sector and why is the informal sector so big in Bolivia based on the INE Households Survey 2005. Finally, the chapter assesses the implication of a big informal sector on economic growth and the provision of public goods. In this chapter, the concept of informality used includes workers as well as firms operating in the informal sector.
- The second chapter is based on the qualitative analysis of focus group interviews of micro and small firms. It investigates a range of constraints that currently limit their productivity focusing on inputs (financial, physical, and human capital) and production (technology and competition). The focus group analysis also identifies constraints posed by the operational, regulatory, and institutional environment, as they affect infrastructure, labor, trade and customs regulations, access to courts, and corruption based on the ICA 2006 data for Bolivia.
- The third chapter reports the results of a new micro survey of small firms carried out for the study. The quantitative analysis investigates the determinants of informality, the effects of informality on the profitability for micro, small, and medium firms, and the channels through which formality affects profitability.
- The fourth chapter develops the policy recommendations of the study on formalization and productivity based on the fresh understanding of firms' behavior regarding formality, productivity, and profitability from chapters 2 and 3. The chapter starts with a set of policy recommendations most promising to increase the formalization of micro and small firms and then makes policy recommendations to increase the productivity of micro and small firms in Bolivia. The current strategy and actions undertaken by the government are presented within the framework of the PND.

Notes

[1] See LAC Flagship report on informality, 2007.

CHAPTER 1

The Informal Sector
in Bolivia Today

Understanding informality in Bolivia today is a key to improving income opportunities for the poor. The informal sector is an important provider of job opportunities in Bolivia, particularly for the most vulnerable groups. Thus, understanding the heterogeneity, causes, and effects of informality is a first critical step in designing policies to improve income opportunities for Bolivia's poor people seeking jobs or working in informal micro and small enterprises. The chapter includes five sections. The first one discusses the importance of informality in Bolivia under different definitions and measures. The second section describes the sociodemographic characteristics of informal employees, trying to explain why some demographic groups and business are overrepresented in this sector. The third section looks at factors that explain why informality is so big in Bolivia. The fourth section assesses the relevance of informality on economic growth, governance, and provision of public goods. The last section summarizes the main conclusions.

How Big Is the Informal Sector in Bolivia?

Bolivia's informal sector is one the largest in the region.

According to a productive definition based on worker characteristics and firm size, 77 percent of employment in Bolivia is informal, taking into account workers in both urban and rural areas (Annex 1.1 for a discussion on definitions and measures of informality, including those used in this chapter). This is the highest level in the region where the average share of informal employment is below 60 percent. Nonsalaried workers make up about 30 percent of all Bolivian employment, triple the regional average. However, nonsalaried work is even more dominant in Bolivia's rural areas, where there is a high propensity to organize household productive units; in urban areas only 11 percent of the employed are nonsalaried workers. Self-employment in Bolivia (at 35 percent) is also above the regional average (29 percent), while the proportion of salaried employees working in small firms is among the lowest in the region.

Informality in Bolivia is also among the highest in the region under a legalistic definition based on the right to a retirement pension linked to employment. Only 30 percent of workers are registered in the insurance-based pension system[1]—the lowest in the region along with Paraguay—even though the share of salaried workers having a signed labor contract is not unusually low (40 percent). The reduced coverage of pension systems is related to the high incidence of unskilled self-employment and nonsalaried work, both of which are usually excluded from pension systems in all countries in the region. Furthermore, in spite of being voluntary, the pension system has not been able to attract workers that could easily choose to participate, such as professional and salaried employees in large firms; only a quarter of salaried workers in large firms are covered.

Moreover, Bolivia leads the world in value-added generated by the informal sector as a share of gross domestic product. The production of the informal sector in Bolivia is the largest among the 145 countries evaluated by Schneider (2004), reaching 68 percent of GDP (Figure 1.1). This estimate, obtained using the DYMIMIC and Currency Demand Methods, allows useful comparisons, but may overestimate the incidence of informality, assigning to it the effect of other unknown variables (World Bank 2007; Annex 1.1).

Figure 1.1. Share of the informal sector in GDP in Latin America and other regions

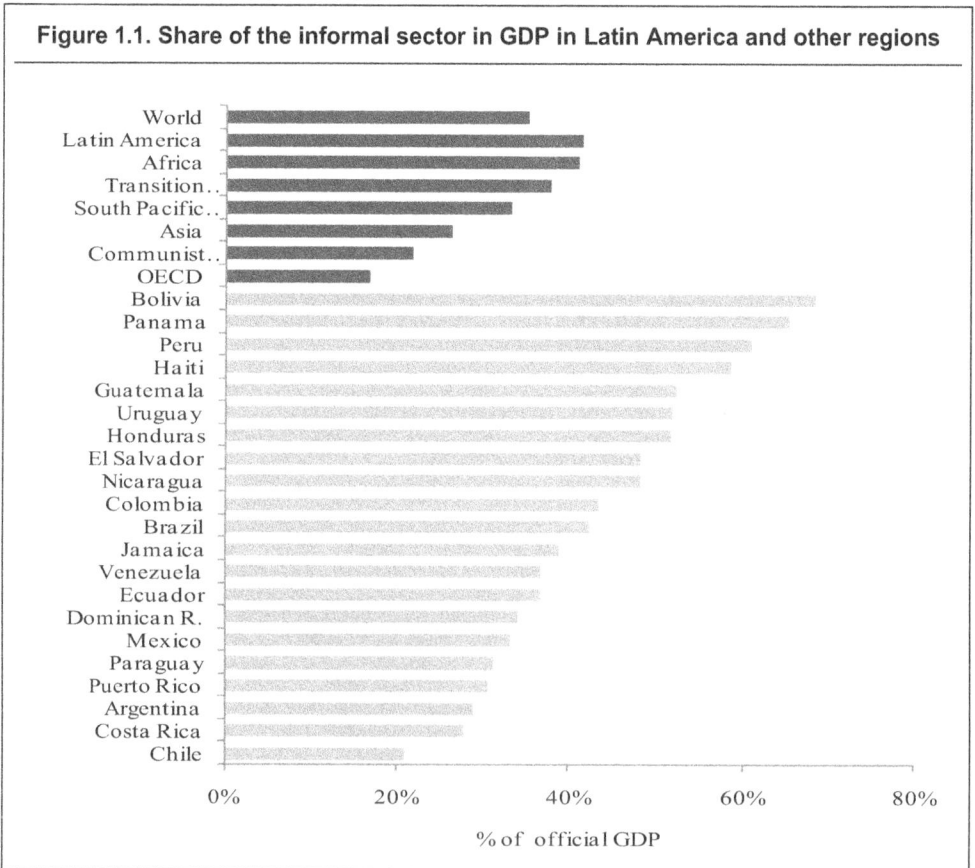

Source: Schneider 2004.

Table 1.1. Distribution of urban employment among formal and informal sectors, by productive and legalistic definitions of informality, 2005 (percentage of total employed population)

Legalistic definition		Productive definition						
		Formal			Informal and domestic			
			Private		Informal			
		Public	Salaried	Non-salaried	Salaried	Non-salaried	Domestic	Total
Formal	Salaried	7.8	8.3		0.4		0.1	16.6
	Non-salaried			0.8		1.9		2.7
Informal	Salaried	2.0	16.4		12.2		3.7	34.3
	Non-salaried			1.7		44.7		46.4
Total		9.8	24.7	2.5	12.6	46.6	3.8	100

Source: INE, EDH 2005.

In the urban informal sector, nonsalaried employment prevails, while salaried employment dominates in the formal sector. Using the productive definition, the informal sector incorporates about 60 percent of the employed labor force in urban areas, of which three-quarters are nonsalaried (Table 1.1). Formal workers are highly concentrated in salaried employment—the public sector and private salaried employment generate about a quarter and two thirds of formal employment, respectively.

The coverage of the pension system is concentrated in the public sector and some medium and large private firms. Considering the legalistic definition based on pension system coverage, informality reaches 80 percent of urban employed labor force. The private formal sector generates about 30 percent of total employment under the productive definition and about 10 percent in the legalistic one. This difference shows that a number of medium and large enterprises that are defined as formal under the productive definition keep their employees out of the pension system. More than three quarters of public employees are affiliated with pension funds, but only a third of workers in the formal sector have pension rights related to employment. Moreover, almost all workers defined as informal under the productive definition are not in the pension system.

The size of the informal sector has been stable in recent years

High informality in Bolivia is not a recent phenomenon. Structural changes introduced in the 1950s spurred a fast urbanization process strengthening the informal sector in the absence of a dynamic private formal sector (Lay 2003). Informality in the mid-1970s generated 57 percent of employment in capital cities, under a productivity definition (before 1999 household surveys were carried out only in capital cities). Informality reached 62 percent of the employed population in the late 1980s, mainly because of the reduction of public sector employment related to the stabilization process started in the mid 1980s, which was not complemented with policies to encourage the private sector development. Jemio (1999) shows that public employment decreased from 26 percent in capital cities in 1985 to 18 percent in 1989.

Since 1990 informality has fluctuated without a definite trend. Between 1997 and 2002, the annual growth of informality in Bolivia was near 0.5 percent and below most countries in the region—extending this result to 2005, the tendency became slightly negative (Figure 1.2). Moreover, in the first half of the 1990s, informality in capital cities stabilized near 58 percent of employed population, fluctuating around this level afterwards (Figure 1.3). This conclusion can be extended to all urban areas in the past ten years using the estimations of urban informality in Yañez and Landa (2007). However, the volatility of informality does not seem to be associated with the economic cycle: Loayza and Rigolini (2006) showed that informality is relatively acyclical in Bolivia, as in other countries with huge informal sectors, such as Peru. In this context, informality fluctuations can be explained by survey errors and methodological changes, which restrict the comparability of surveys over time. The recent reduction of urban informality from 63 percent in 2003–04 to 59 percent in 2005 must be taken with caution.

Figure 1.2. Annual change in informal employment in Latin American countries

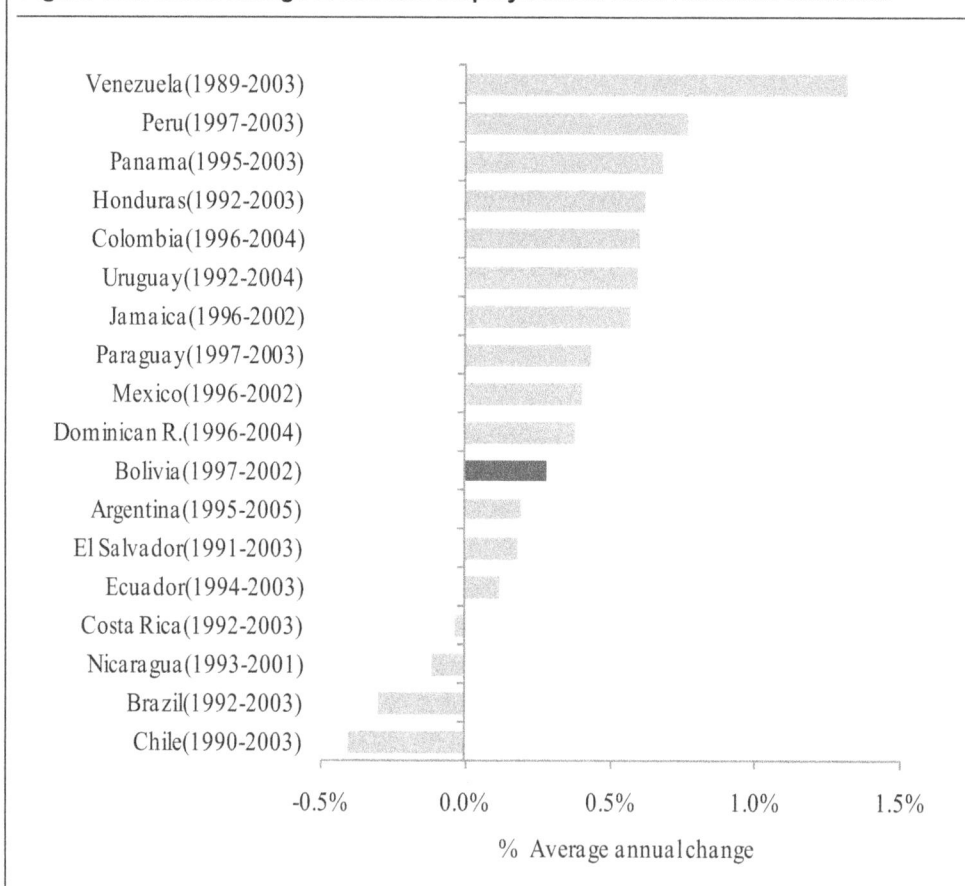

Source: Gasparini and Tornarolli 2007.

Figure 1.3. Share of informal workers in the employed population in Bolivian urban areas, 1989–2005

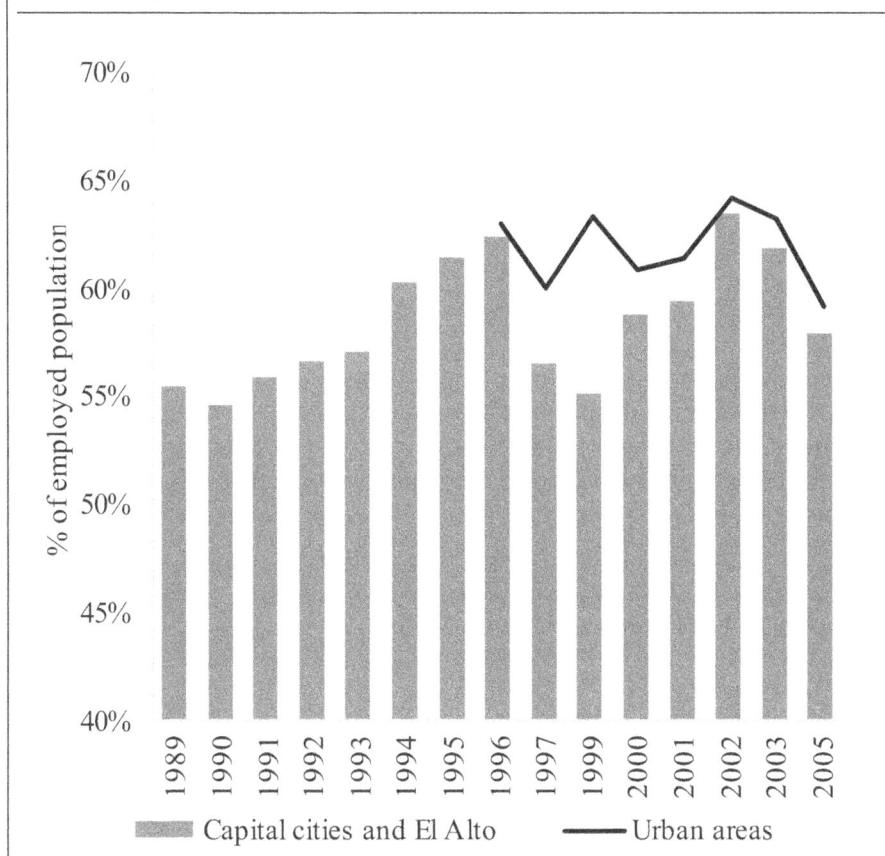

Source: Yañez and Landa 2007; UDAPE 2006; and INE-EDH 2005.
Note: It does not include domestic workers.

Despite the structural trends encouraging informality, the private formal sector was able to create enough employment to avoid further growth of the informal sector. Those structural changes include the migration process, which contributed to the rise in urbanization from 58 percent of the population in 1992 to 62 percent in 2001. In addition, public employment in capital cities was gradually reduced from 18 percent of the employed population in 1990 to less than 10 percent in 2005; nonetheless, the absolute number of public employees has increased by 19 percent between 1995 and 2007. Employment generated by previously existing firms has stagnated since 1995, according to the private employment index estimated by the National Statistics Office (INE) using the outdated administrative registries of the Ministry of Labor. The increase in private labor is linked to the creation of new formal private firms—those with more than four workers—which has compensated these structural changes, avoiding a sustained growth of informality.

Who Is in The Informal Sector?

Informal workers are heterogeneous

The informal sector attracts all kinds of workers, including successful entrepreneurs as well as those disadvantaged in the formal sector. Using the productive definition, informality reaches about 45 percent of nonindigenous males between 30 and 40 years old who have finished at least secondary education, a sector not obviously related to informality. However, some sectors are significantly overrepresented in the informal sector, mainly because informality offers flexible job opportunities to people who may find restrictions in the formal labor market. Overrepresented sectors include people with modest education, women, indigenous people, the young, and the elderly, usually presenting high poverty prevalence (Monterrey 2003). In addition the informal sector offers an opportunity to be independent—about 65 percent of workers express a desire to be independent.

The high dispersion of labor income, especially among nonsalaried workers, also reflects the heterogeneity of the informal sector. Using a legalistic definition, Landa et al. (2007) showed that the average income of the self-employed, which are mostly informal, and that of informal salaried workers are close, but the income distribution of the self-employed is more dispersed, consistent with international evidence (Figure 1.4).

Figure 1.4. Distribution of hourly earnings for salaried workers in the formal and informal sectors and self-employed workers, 2005

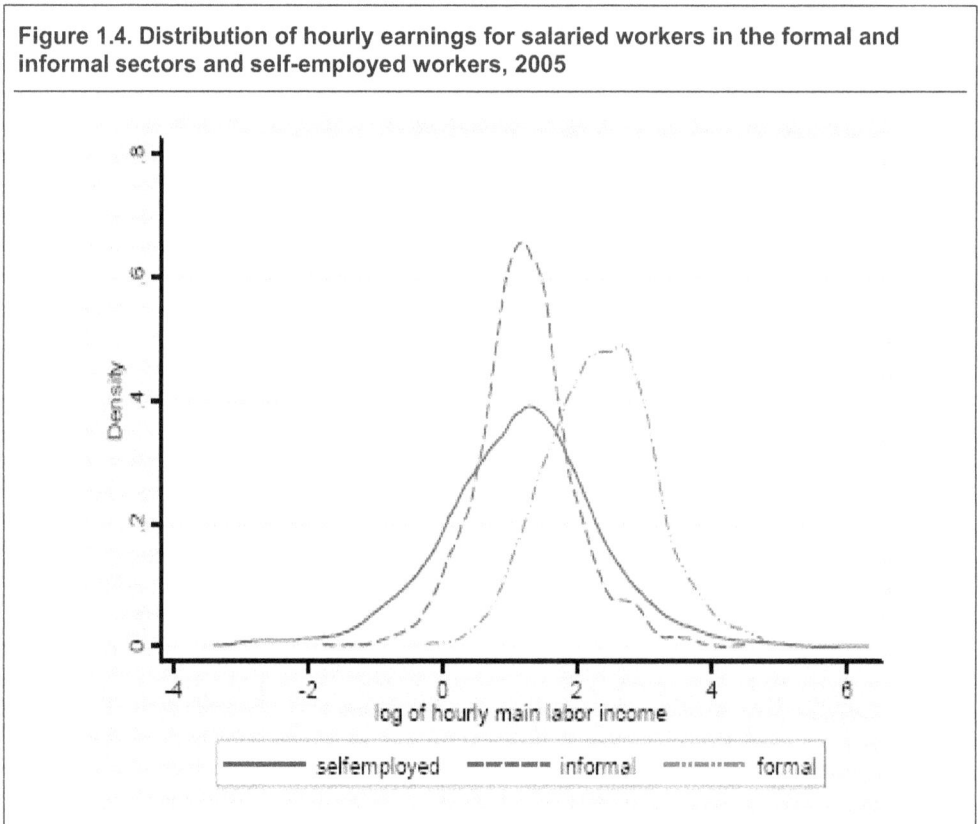

Source: Landa et al. 2007.

Figure 1.5. Distribution of workers by sector and labor income quintile, 2005

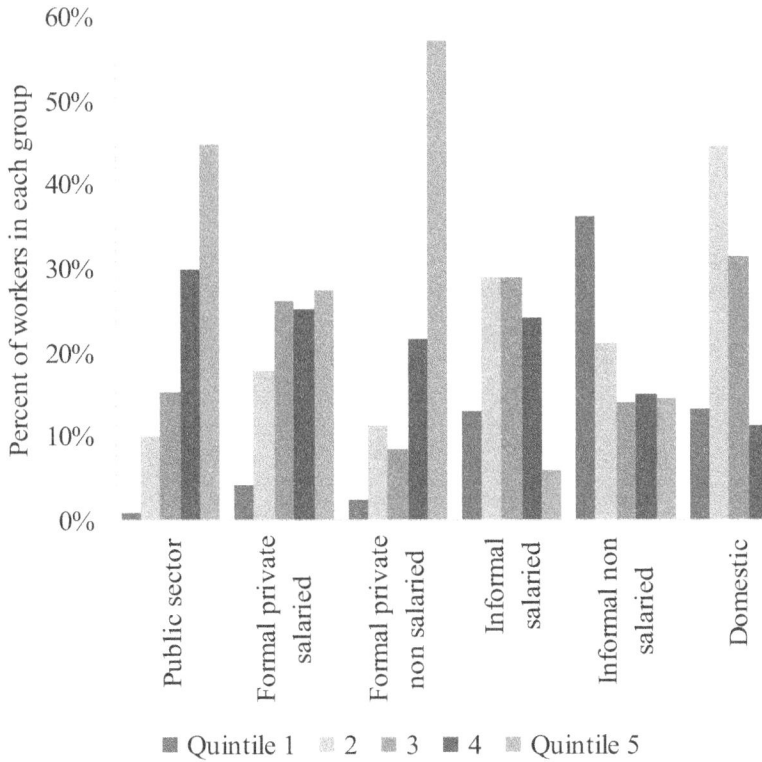

Source: INE-EDH 2005.

This implies that informal nonsalaried employment covers a diversity of people, including those successful self-employed who accumulated enough experience and capital to reach high labor incomes, as well as those unsuccessful self-employed with few options to improve their earnings. The last case is more common: 35 percent of informal nonsalaried workers are in the lowest labor income quintile, while the rest are uniformly distributed among the other quintiles (Figure 1.5).

Salaried workers seem to be more homogeneous than nonsalaried workers, especially in the informal sector. Formal salaried employees have an earnings advantage over informal salaried employees, but the distribution of their incomes is more dispersed (Figure 1.4). This is at least partially explained by the higher earnings of public employees compared to other formal private employees. Most public employees are concentrated in the highest quintiles, increasing the intergroup inequality as well as the inequality among all formal salaried employees. However, these income differences mostly reflect employees' attribute differences, in particular education: for example, public employees have, on average, four more years of education than those working in the private formal sector and six more years of education than informal employees.

Certain groups tend more to be informal

While three-quarters of the population without education is informal, only one-third of the population with higher education is. While formal employees have an average of 12 years of schooling (11 if public sector employees are not included), employees in the informal sector have hardly finished primary school—8.4 years of education on average (Annexes 1.2 and 1.3). A high level of education reduces the likelihood of being informal, and tertiary education is particularly important. Moreover, the formal sector is more important for people between 20 and 30 years old, because the formal sector tends to hire people with higher education, in particular professionals. Nevertheless, informal employment in this age range is not reduced, because the increase in formal employment is mostly linked to people who were previously studying and out of the labor market. This is due to the preference of the formal employers for better-educated people and the preference of better-educated workers for salaried jobs; two thirds of workers without education prefer an independent job, while only half of educated people desire this kind of job. Additionally, education better explains earnings for formal workers than for self-employed informal workers, where it has practically no role (Tannuri-Pianto and Pianto 2003).

Women are strongly represented in the informal sector. Only one third of the formal workers are women, and this proportion decreases to one quarter if the public sector, more gender balanced, is excluded. Women's lesser formal employment is partially due to their lower educational achievement and a disadvantaging labor regulation. However, this factor does not fully explain the high informality of women, in particular their disproportionate propensity to be self-employed—80 percent of women working informally are nonsalaried. This trend may be the result of women's persistent family responsibilities, which often interfere with formal work schedules (Tannuri-Pianto and Pianto 2003). The flexibility of self-employment allows women to balance their need to complement family income and take care of their children and other family members (World Bank 2005b). Figure 1.6 shows that women's informal self-employment is more sensitive to marital status than men's. In addition, women are more likely to be informal if the spouse is a formal employee. In a related way, the elasticity of women's working hours is negatively related to their spouse's wage variations (Mercado and Rios 2005).

Indigenous people are also overrepresented in the informal sector. Indigenous people are well represented in the informal sector, whether indigenous status is measured by self-identification or native tongue. Two thirds of self-identified indigenous people are informal, compared with half of all the nonindigenous (Annexes 1.2 and 1.3). However, this overrepresentation is also linked with a low level of education among indigenous people. At high levels of education (completed secondary and tertiary schooling), both indigenous and nonindigenous groups have similar levels of informality (Figure 1.7). Moreover, under the legalistic definition there is no evidence of a relation between ethnicity and informality, once other factors, including education, are controlled for (World Bank 2007). In the highlands, ethnic discrimination does not explain income gaps in urban workers, although in the lowlands this factor cannot be ruled out (Villegas and Nuñez 2005).

Figure 1.6. Share of informal self-employment in employment, by gender and marital status, 2005

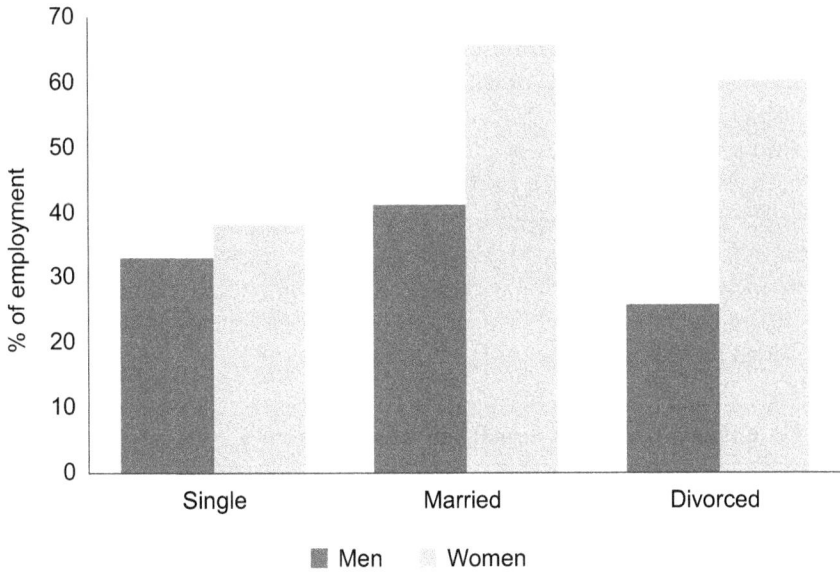

Source: INE, EDH 2005.

Figure 1.7. Share of informal employment in all employment, by education and ethnicity, 2005

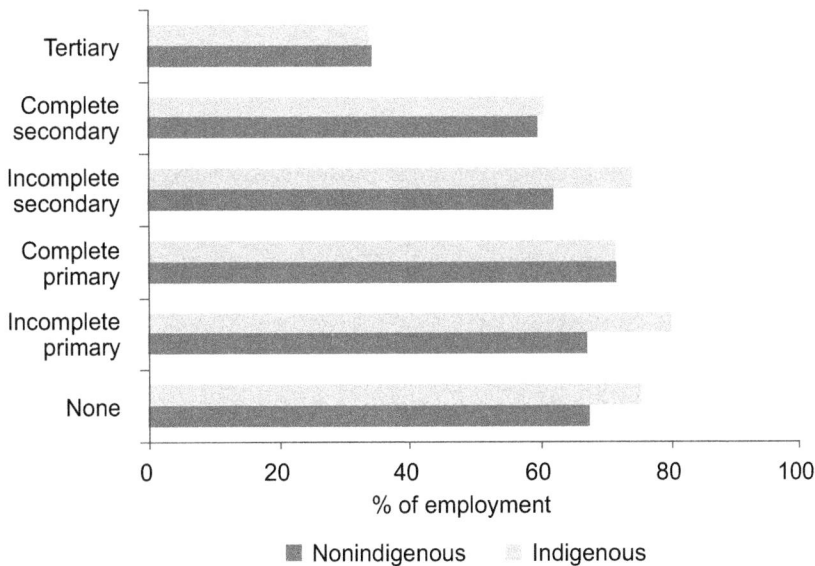

Source: INE, EDH 2005.
Note: Indigenous by native tongue.

Young people often enter the labor market through the informal sector. About two thirds of workers between 15 and 19 years of age are informal because young people tend to have lower education and to work with their families (Figures 1.8 and 1.9). Additionally, the flexibility of informal employment allows young people to study and evaluate other labor alternatives. Self-employment is very important among young people in Bolivia, generating one third of their employment. In other developing countries, such as Argentina, Brazil, Mexico, and the Dominican Republic, young people usually enter the labor market as salaried workers, formal or informal, while they build up enough financial or human capital to start their own enterprise (World Bank 2007). This suggests that in Bolivia an important part of self-employment is related with activities that require small physical or human capital and therefore present lower barriers to entry and higher exit rates. For workers between 20 and 30 years old, there is an increase in the formal sector employment, as some who stayed in school earlier have completed their education and are entering the labor market in higher-skilled jobs, as mentioned before.

Figure 1.8. Employment in the formal and informal sectors, by workers' age, 2005

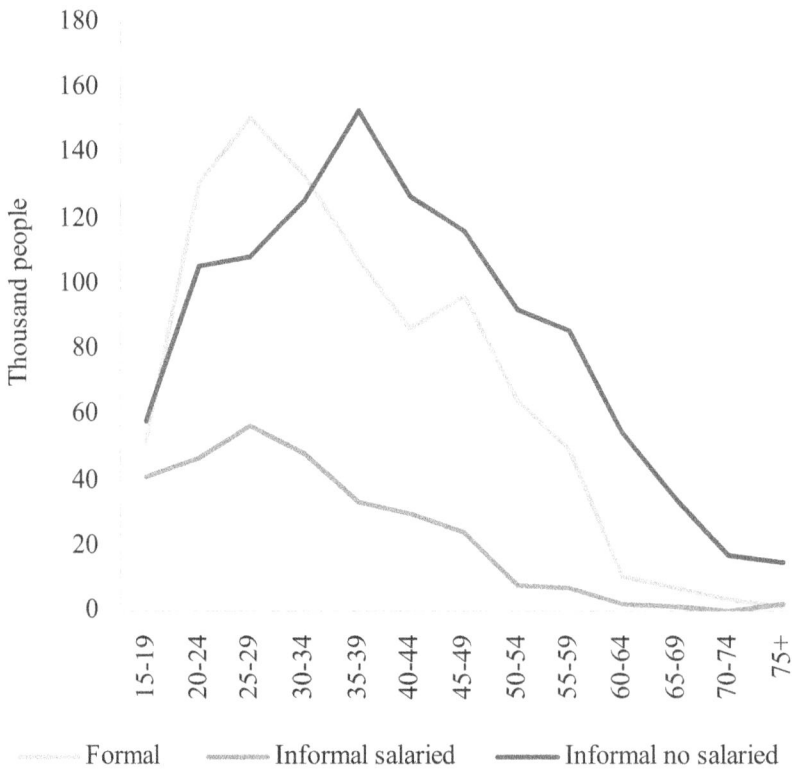

Source: INE, EDH 2005.

Figure 1.9. Share of informal self-employment in all employment, by age and gender, 2005

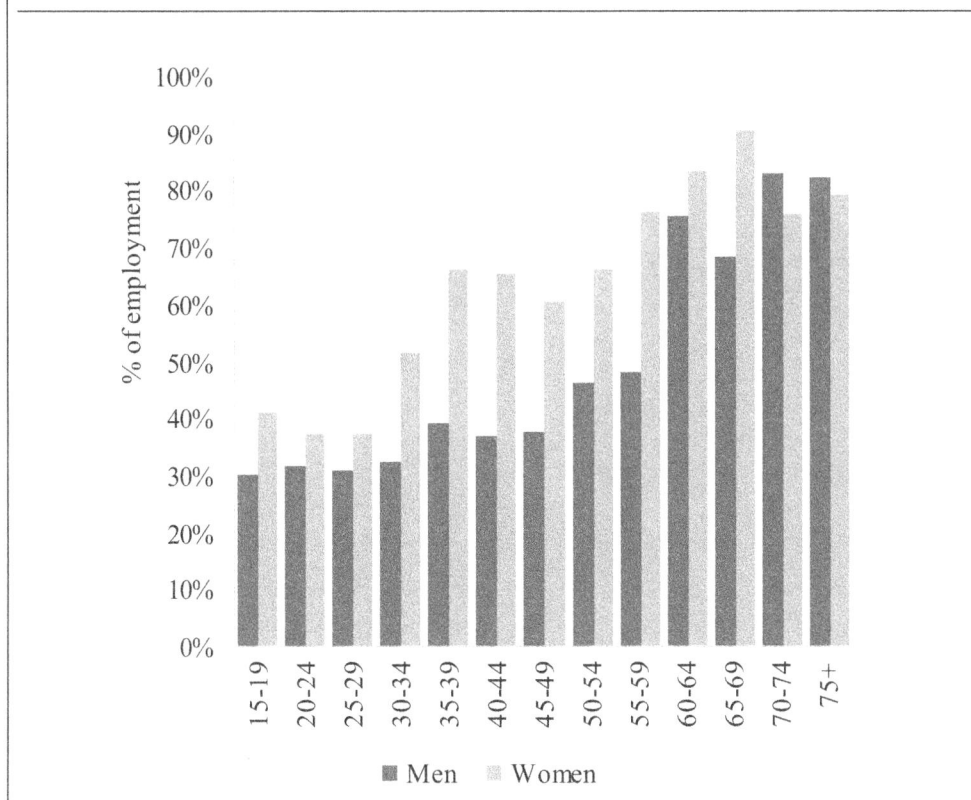

Source: INE, EDH 2005.

Older workers often turn to informal self-employment. At the age of 30 years, salaried employment, especially informal salaried employment, quickly falls in favor of self-employment. This phenomenon is linked to the massive migration of women between 30 and 40 years old to self-employment because of their growing family responsibilities. Male self-employment follows a slower growing trend until the formal age of retirement, between 60 and 65. Older men tend to turn to self-employment because they have accumulated the required financial and human capital to start their own enterprise or because they have been displaced by younger and better-educated workers. Finally, retirement triggers another important change in favor of self-employment, because those retired from formal and informal activities migrate to informal self-employment to continue generating incomes for their families in a more flexible sector.

Figure 1.10. Average number of years spent in employment, by sector

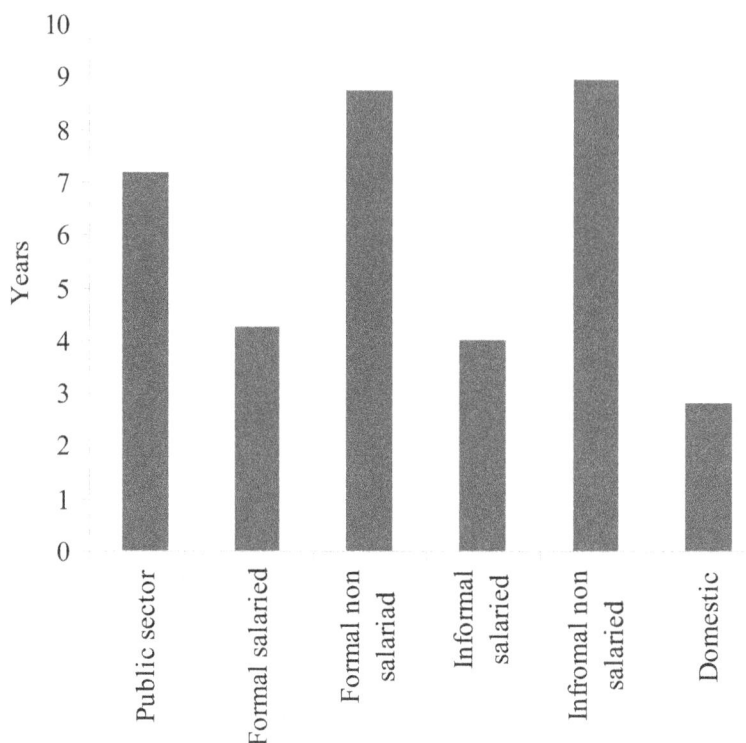

Source: INE, EDH 2005.

Workers face a slow transition between the formal and the informal sector. Workers move slowly between the formal and informal sectors, even after long periods of time (Landa et al. 2007). They also tend to remain in the same work category (employed or self-employed) inside each sector. However, there is no strong evidence of labor market segmentation between the formal and the informal sector. Figure 1.10 shows that the time worked in the same firm is similar for salaried and self-employed workers in each sector. In addition, informal employees have more labor stability: while two thirds of informal workers remain in the same occupation more than two years, only half of formal ones do Landa and Yañez (2007)[2]. These findings do not support the common vision of a volatile informal job and can be explained by the unusually high level of informal self-employment in Bolivia. The level of education in the formal sector and the experience accumulated in the informal sector increase the mobility inside each sector, but do not increase mobility between sectors (Jimenez and Jimenez 2000).

Informality is concentrated in some sectors and types of firms

Public administration, education, health, and extractive industries are the most formal sectors, but they generate only a small part of total employment. The public sector is highly involved in these industries, either directly or through large-scale private initiatives in education and extractive industries, which are easily identified by the authorities (Figure 1.11). Furthermore, users of private education require formalization of education institutions. In the health sector, where formality is also high, men are more likely than women to be informal workers—a reverse of the usual trend. Informality of male health workers is about 40 percent, while informality among women is close to 30 percent. Women tend to work in support activities in formal institutions while men, who are most often doctors, have more flexibility to provide services independently. However, all these sectors generated only 14 percent of total employment in urban areas, mostly for those with a relatively high level of education.

The most informal sectors are commerce and transport, which generate an important portion of total employment. Commerce employs one-third of women and 16 percent of men, with informality rates of 95 percent and 75 percent, respectively. Almost all transport sector workers are men with an informality rate close to 75 percent. These sectors are characterized by low entry barriers and hence can provide income opportunities for workers in transition to the formal economy. Most workers in these sectors engage in small-scale activities and self-employment, making formalization and enforcement very difficult. Currently, only municipalities have a limited enforcement power on small-scale commerce, while transport activities can be carried out almost without restrictions. The special tax regimes applied to these sectors—a simplified regime and unified regime, respectively—have allowed them to avoid tax payments. Commerce and restaurants seem to be more attractive for women because of time flexibility and lower educational requirements.

Informality reaches half of all people working in manufacturing and construction. Both sectors show wide disparities in gender. In manufacturing, the share of men and women holding jobs is similar (20 percent of men and 13 percent of women), but informality rates differ markedly (half of men and three quarters percent of women). In construction, women are not commonly employed; 15 percent of men work in construction, with an informality rate close to 50 percent. The relative formality of these sectors is not related to education levels, because the average years of schooling needed to enter either sector are close to those observed in transport and commerce. Moreover, the formality of these sectors seems to be related to the large scale needed to carry out most manufacturing and construction activities profitably.

The smaller the firm, the more likely it is to be informal. Figure 1.12 shows a negative relationship between the number of workers in a firm and its formality, measured by their registration in the Tax Services. While 80 percent of people working in firms with four or fewer workers say that these establishments do not have a tax identification number (NIT), more than 90 percent of those working in firms with more than 50 people declare that these establishments have a NIT. This is because formality may be considered a normal good in productive processes (Maloney 2006). Large firms can take advantage of some of the benefits of formality and face its cost more easily than small firms, and large firms are easier for authorities to identify and control.

Figure 1.11. Share of informal employment in all employment, by economic sector and gender, 2005

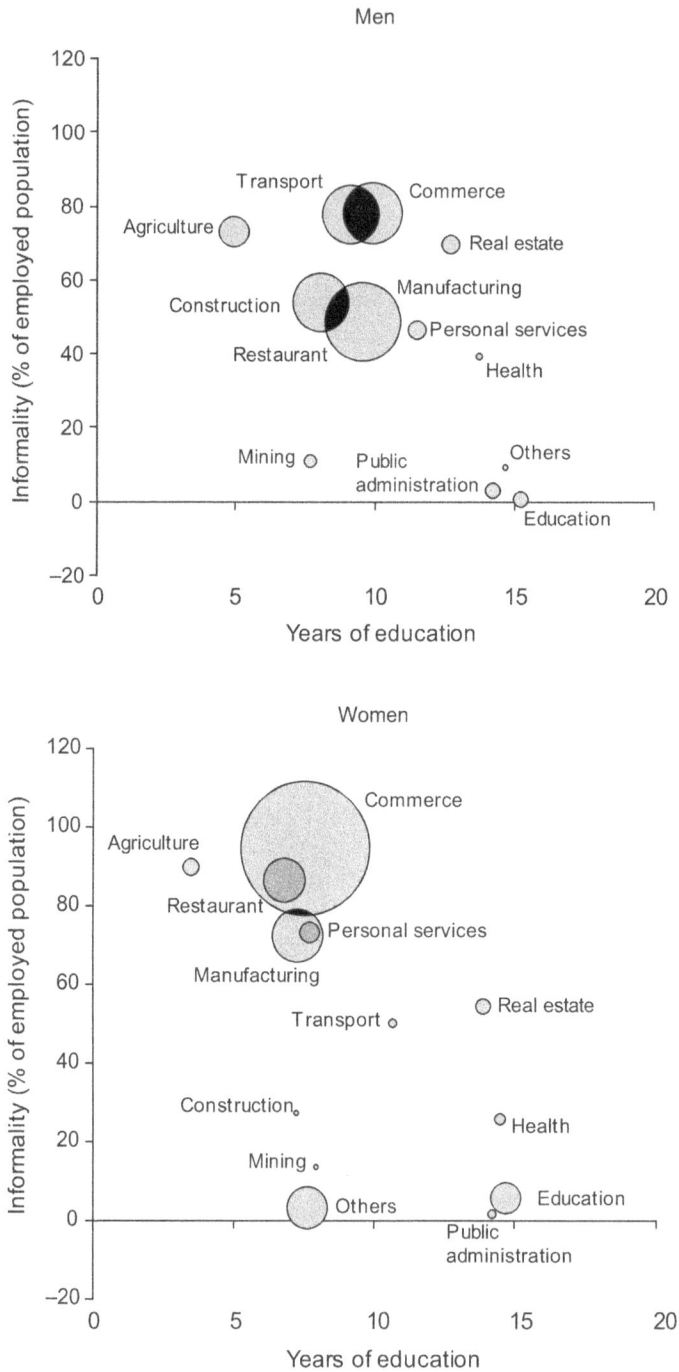

Men

Women

Figure 1.12. Share of informal employment in all employment, by size of firm, 2005

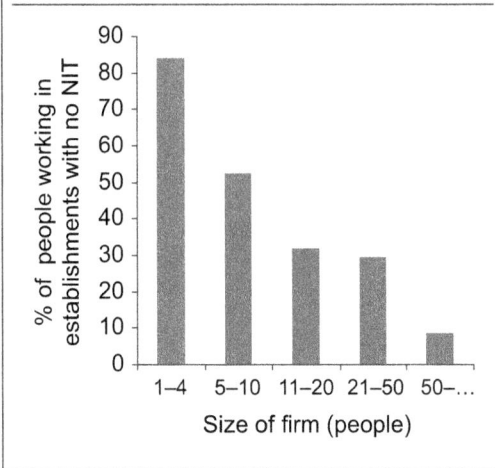

Size of firm (people)

Source: INE, EDH 2005.

Furthermore, large firms are more prone to have formal labor relationships with their employees. Table 1.2 shows that almost all employees working in firms with one to four people are not affiliated to any pension fund and do not have formal contracts, while half of people working in firms with more than 50 workers have a formal contract and are affiliated with pension funds.

Why Is the Informal Sector so Big?

Informality is a rational choice

Informality is attractive to many as it allows more flexibility and independence. Factors such as the poor quality of services provided to the formal sector and the flexibility, independence, and opportunity available in the informal sector make informality attractive for some sectors of the population. Figure 1.13 shows that independent jobs are preferred in all labor categories except domestic workers and public employees. Moreover, the desire to be independent is higher among already independent workers than among salaried ones, in particular those employed in the formal sector. As women are far more concentrated in the informal self-employment option and their preference is also to be independent, they appear to be nearer their desired state than men. However, these findings do not allow discarding the hypothesis that some segments of the population enter the informal sector involuntarily and remain far from their optimal preferences (Mercado and Rios, 2005). A quarter of independent workers desire to be salaried workers and two thirds of informal salaries employees report that they chose their occupation because they could not find another job. Only one third of formal salaried workers chose their job (World Bank, 2007).

Table 1.2. Share of workers covered by labor contracts and pension funds, by firm size, 2005 (percentage of salaried employment)

Number of workers in the firm	Coverage of blue-collar and white-collar employees				
	None	Only pension fund	Only contract	Both	Total
1-4 workers	30.4	2.5	0.6	0.3	33.8
4-10 workers	18.5	2.3	0.9	2.4	24.2
11-20 workers	7.3	3.0	0.6	2.9	13.8
21-50 workers	5.5	1.5	0.9	4.0	12.0
50-... workers	4.5	1.8	1.2	8.7	16.3
Total	66.3	11.1	4.3	18.3	100.0

Source: INE, EDH 2005.

Figure 1.13. Share of formal and informal workers who desire being independent or salaried, by sector, 2005

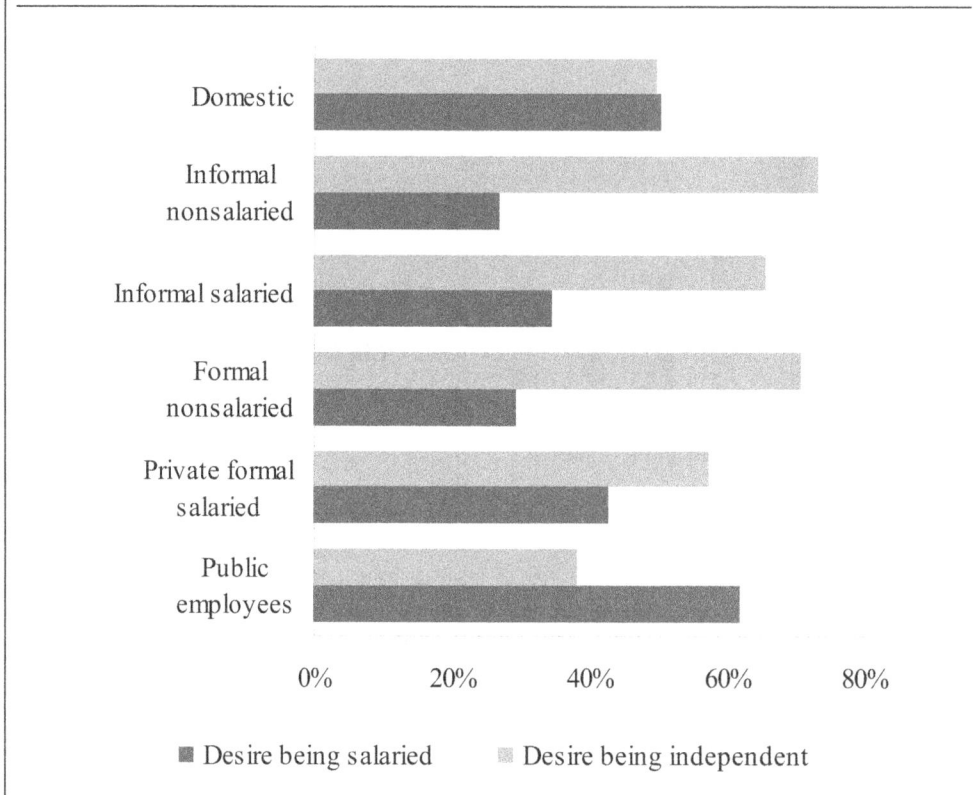

Source: INE, EDH 2005.

An analysis of the main costs and benefits of being formal suggests that both specific and more general factors need to be considered. The second section of Table 1.3 summarizes the main costs and benefits of being formal in Bolivia. Regulation costs, in particular those related to labor and tax collection, are more important than tax rates in constraining participation in the formal sector. Moreover, the benefits of being in the formal sector are constrained by the weak capacity of public institutions to apply regulations and to provide market support services. For instance, better access to foreign markets and government procurement is an important benefit of being formal, but only for a handful of markets—the nontradable sectors not linked with public purchases do not share this benefit. Better access to finance is another important benefit of being formal, despite the growing access to microfinance for some informal micro and small enterprises.

Table 1.3. Costs and benefits of being formal

Cost	Benefit
Factors affecting specific groups	
Flexibility losses	*Better protection for workers*
Work inflexibility in the formal sector implies a restriction for some groups of people, in particular women and young people. Work in the informal sector is far more flexible.	Nevertheless, this benefit is relative because public institutions in Bolivia have been unable to ensure an effective set of minimum protections to most workers. In addition, the quality of the services provided to formal workers is poor.
Most infant firms are informal in order to have more flexibility to move their factors to other sectors, while formal entrepreneurs face important restrictions to reallocate factors among sectors.	*Economies of scale*
	Formality is a normal good in the production process, which is acquired when the firm grows.
Factor affecting all Bolivians	
Barriers to registering	*Avoiding penalties of being informal*
Formalization red tape is still expensive and time consuming, excluding small enterprises from the formal sector.	Weak public institutions have been unable to ensure regulation accomplishment.
	Access to market support services
Other regulations linked with firm's management	Public institutions do not provide adequate market support services. Judicial procedures are complex, and they do not provide enough property rights protection.
Most regulations are expensive and complex, in particular those related to labor regulation and tax collections.	
Taxes	*Access to foreign markets and government procurement*
In Bolivia, the value added and corporate income tax rates are not unusually high but transaction taxes increases the tax burden well above regional average.	Only some sectors can take advantage of these benefits.
	Access to finance
	Formal firms have better access to finance, but microfinance is improving informal sector access. [a]

Note: a. And also has a sizable positive effect in poverty, which has more prevalence in the informal sector (Mosley 1999).

Many firms perceive that the costs of formalization are not offset by the benefits, giving firms few incentives to comply with the procedures. Procedure-complying costs and benefits may vary according for example to the type of firm or on the public agency enforcing the procedure. For instance, at the municipal level, where enforcement is stronger than at the central level, firms register in their municipal government to avoid penalties of being informal and to comply with the law (Figure 1.14). Similarly, larger firms may be more subject to inspection than smaller firms; those issues are explored in more detail in the next two chapters. Hence, by increasing the productive benefits of formalization and increasing the enforcement for not formalizing, authorities may be able to give specific incentives for informal micro and small firms to become formal.

The burden of regulation reduces the appeal of formality

The heavy regulation of formal firms contributes to the high informality in Bolivia. The regulatory complexity affecting formal firms has been blamed as one of the main causes of informality in Bolivia (World Bank 2001 and 2005a). Moreover, in a cross-country study including Bolivia, Loayza et al. (2005) show that increased burden of labor and product market regulation—entry, trade, financial, bankruptcy and contract enforcement regulation—leads to an expansion of informality.

Figure 1.14. Firms' ranking of reasons to formalize at the municipal level—IFC scorecards

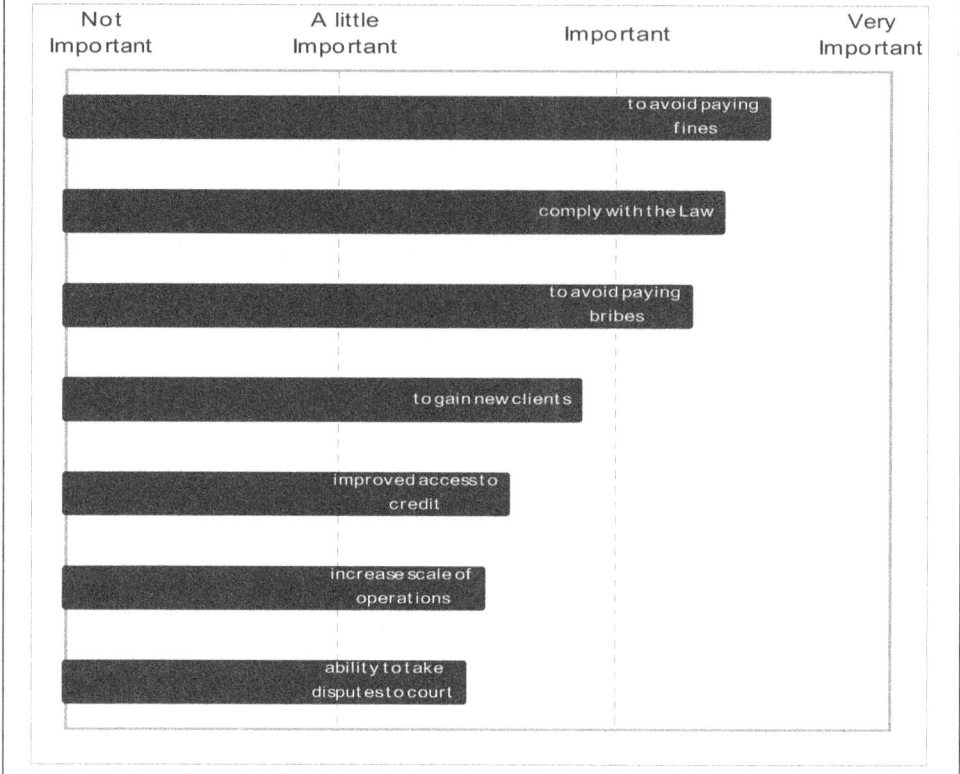

| Not Important | A little Important | Important | Very Important |

- to avoid paying fines
- comply with the Law
- to avoid paying bribes
- to gain new clients
- improved access to credit
- increase scale of operations
- ability to take disputes to court

Source: IFC Municipal Scorecards Report for Bolivia 2007.
Note: Responding firms are registered firms at the municipal level.

Currently, Bolivia's highly restrictive regulation is only topped by República Bolivariana de Venezuela and Haiti in the region—Bolivia is ranked 113 out of 175 countries included in the *Doing Business* report (World Bank and IFC 2006), while Haiti and República Bolivariana de Venezuela are ranked 139 and 165, respectively. However, Bolivia's results in the *Doing Business 2007* report are not uniform (Figure 1.14).

On some issues, such as labor regulation and tax collection, Bolivia is ranked among the lowest in the world, while in other areas, such as getting credit, dealing with licenses, and closing a business, Bolivia ranks better than most countries in the region. For example: Bolivia's time to close a business is 1.8 years on average, close to OECD countries; the costs of closing a business is 15 percent of income per capita, a little below the regional average of 16 percent, although doubling the OECD average; and the recovery rate, which illustrates how many cents on the dollar claimants recover from the insolvent firm, is 39 percent, above the regional average (26 percent) and about half of the OECD average.

Figure 1.15. Summary of the regulatory burden in Bolivia

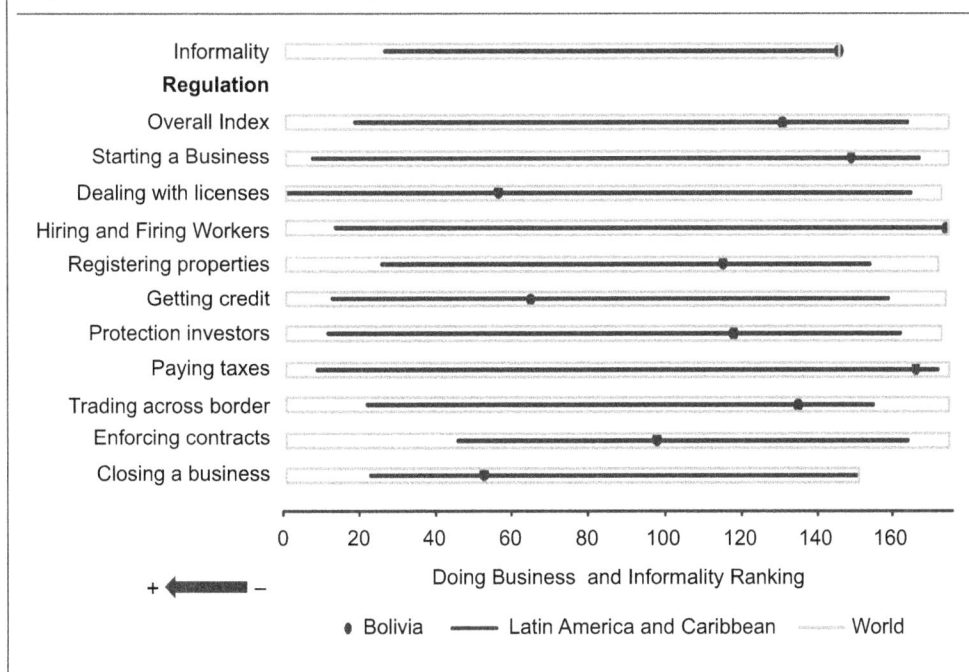

Source: World bank and IFC 2006; Schneider 2004.
Note: Does not include countries with missing data.

Procedural constraints to formalization

Formalization is severely constrained by costs and procedures associated with setting up a business in Bolivia. To allow a valid international comparison, Doing Business 2007 assess the costs and procedures to start up a limited liability company in a sector with no special tax treatments and no incentives to investors with a capital equivalent to 10 times the per capita GNI—about US$10 thousand in the case of Bolivia. In this context, according to the report, the minimum capital requirement—US$32 or 3.8 percent of per capita GNI—is not an important constraint to formalization in Bolivia, being well bellow the regional average that is close to 18 percent (Table 1.4). However, registry costs and procedures are an important constraint: at least 50 days are needed to complete 15 procedures with a total cost close to 140 percent of GNI (Bs 10,900) that is well above the regional average of 48 percent of GNI. Moreover, these costs can be higher due to other regulations applied to specific sectors, such as environmental cards, liquor licenses, and sanitary registry (Ministry of Labor 2006). This hurdle often discourages entrepreneurs' willingness to formalize and to pool with others to scale up production or undertake bigger projects (The following chapters elaborate on the consequences of these restrictions over productivity).

Table 1.4. Costs and procedures to set up a business in Latin American countries

	Procedures number	Duration days	Cost % GNI per capita	Min. Capital % GNI per capita
Argentina	15	32	12.1	5.6
Bolivia	**15**	**50**	**140.6**	**3.8**
Brazil	17	152	9.9	0
Chile	9	27	9.8	0
Colombia	13	44	19.8	0
Costa Rica	11	77	23.5	0
Ecuador	14	65	31.8	7.7
El Salvador	10	26	75.6	119.7
Mexico	8	27	14.2	12.5
Nicaragua	6	39	131.6	0
Panama	7	19	23.9	0
Paraguay	17	74	136.8	0
Peru	10	72	32.5	0
Uruguay	10	43	44.2	183.3
Venezuela, R. B. de	16	141	25.4	0
LAC	10.2	73.3	48.1	18.1
OECD	6.2	16.6	5.3	36.1

Source: World Bank and IFC 2006.

Most of the registry costs are associated with the preparation of the article of incorporation, the bylaws, the constitutional act and the opening balance sheet. Even if the procedures with all public agencies, FundEmpresa and the AFPs were cost-free, opening up a formal firm in Bolivia would still be highly expensive—130 percent of GNI—mainly due to the high lawyer and accountant costs required to prepare the article of incorporation, the bylaws, and the constitutional act (Table 1.5). Bolivian law stipulates that these documents—as every other legal document—must be prepared by an attorney, independently of the enterprise characteristic, and applying the fares schedule of the lawyers association. The cost of this single procedure is equivalent to the annual income of an average Bolivian. Additionally, this contract must be validated by a public notary, who charges an average of 13 percent of the GNI per capita. A charge must also be paid when preparing the opening financial balance. In Ecuador and Peru similar procedures are requested, but at a significantly lower cost: 19 percent (US$500) and 8 percent (US$200) of GNI, respectively. On the other hand, in Argentina, Chile, Mexico, and Colombia it is only required to validate the contract signatures by a public notary partially explaining why the cost to set up a new business in these countries is below 20 percent of their GNI per capita. However, in Bolivia, it is frequent not to apply the fares established by the lawyers association, allowing some small entrepreneurs to obtain the required document at a lower cost.

Table 1.5. Detail of costs and procedures to formally set up a business in Bolivia

	Days	Cost Bs	Cost US$	Cost % of GNI
1. Check uniqueness of name	1	0	0	0
2. Draw article of incorporation	1	7,800	975	101
3. Notarize the article of incorporation	1	1,000	125	13
4. Publish company deed in a national newspaper	2	50	6	1
5. Preparation of opening balance sheet	1	1,000	125	13
6. Seal of opening balance sheet	1	50	6	1
7. Register at National Tax Service	1	0	0	0
8. Obtain the municipal business license (La Paz)	1	0	0	0
9. Municipal government inspection (La Paz)	7	0	0	0
10. Obtain evidence of bank deposit	0	0	0	0
11. Register company at the registry of commerce	9	584	73	8
12. Register at appropriate chamber of commerce of industry	1	320	40	4
13. Register for national health insurance	20	45	6	1
14. Register at Minister of Labor	1	50	6	1
15. Register employees with Pension Fund Management	3	0	0	0
TOTAL	50	10,899	1,362	141

Source: World Bank and IFC 2006.

Setting up a business in Bolivia involves several agencies and cumbersome procedures. The Labor Ministry, the National Health Institution, the Tax Service, and municipal governments, as well as the AFPs and FundEmpresa—the private operators in charge of pension system and registry of commerce in Bolivia—all apply independent procedures and there is no information exchange or coordination among them (ILD 2007). However, the registries at the National Health Institution and at FundEmpresa are the most burdensome procedures consuming 9 and 20 days respectively, despite the fact that they do not include in situ inspections, like some procedures demanded by municipalities—only 7 days are required to obtain a municipal business license in La Paz. Thus, the time needed to open a business in Bolivia could be substantially reduced consolidating some procedures and improving others, in particular health insurance registry procedure. In addition, these services are highly concentrated in capital cities, increasing the cost of setting up a new business in other areas. The Ministry of Labor only has an office in La Paz; the tax service and the National Health Institution have offices in capital cities; the FundEmpresa has offices in capital cities, El Alto, and Montero; and AFPs have offices in capital cities and Riberalta. However, if these procedures are not simplified before, the effort to increase their coverage to intermediate cities could by difficult and expensive.

In recent years, in the context of an official red tape simplification program, the registry of commerce and the municipal business license were significantly improved. Under the 2001 initiative denominated *Sistema Boliviano de Productividad y*

Competitividad (SBPC) executed by the Productivity and Competitiveness Unit (UPC) as its operative branch, a number of procedures were revised and enhanced. In 2001, the registry of commerce was granted in a concession to a private operator named FundEmpresa (*Fundación para el Desarrollo Empresarial*). This institution has doubled the number of registries at the registry of commerce between 2002 and 2005 by decentralizing the procedure, which was previously applied only in La Paz, and reducing significantly the time required to check the name and registry from more than 50 days to only 10 days (DECMA 2006). However, many firms still ignore the existence of the institution or its role. At the municipal level, the Entrepreneurial Card (*Tarjeta Empresarial),* which allows local firms to work with their municipalities through a simple registration process, was created. Other initiatives included the *Guía Nacional de Trámites,* accessible through the Internet and centralizing the existing administrative procedures at the central, prefectural, and municipal levels. Continuing these efforts, another important simplification implemented afterward was the reduction of time to obtain the municipal business license in some municipalities supported by the IFC. In the municipal governments where this measure was applied, the number of licenses issued increased; for instance, between 2004 and 2005, La Paz, Tarija, Montero, and Trinidad registered an increase in the number of licenses granted of 8 percent, 52 percent, 21 percent, and 65 percent respectively. However, this time has varied widely because only a handful of municipalities implemented the program. Obtaining a business license requires five months in Oruro, but less than five days in La Paz, Sucre, and El Alto (IFC 2007).

Tax regulation is still burdensome

Despite recent improvements in tax administration, tax regulation is still burdensome. In recent years the tax service has made efforts to improve its collection and to simplify some procedures. As a result of these reforms, Bolivia is relatively well ranked in the perception of simplicity and transparency of the tax system (41 of 117 countries in 2005) and in its impact on the incentives to work and invest (55 of 125 countries in 2006) (WEF 2005 and 2006). However, tax regulation is still cumbersome. Tax payments amount to 80 percent of gross profits while the regional average reaches 50 percent (Table 1.6). Time required to pay taxes reached 1,080 hours per year in Bolivia compared to the regional average of 430 hours.

Due to the transaction tax, the tax burden is high though the value added and the corporate income tax rates are not. The tax system was modernized under the economic reforms initiated in the mid-1980s, although a personal income tax was not introduced and the system relies on indirect taxes. Value added (VAT) and corporate income tax rates do not appear excessive compared to other countries: the corporate income tax rate (25 percent) is modest in relation to other countries and the VAT (14.9 percent) is close to the regional average (World Bank 2005). However, the tax burden is well above the regional standard due to the transaction tax that amounts to 63 percent of gross profits and 45 percent excluding corporate income tax accreditation—the amount paid under the corporate income tax may be considered as payment of the transaction tax (Doing Business 2007).

Table 1.6. Tax regulation burden in Latin American countries

	Payments number	Time hours	Tax payable % gross profit
Argentina	34	615	116.8
Bolivia	41	1080	80.3
Brazil	23	2600	71.7
Chile	10	432	26.3
Colombia	68	456	82.8
Costa Rica	41	402	83.0
Ecuador	8	600	34.9
El Salvador	66	224	27.4
Mexico	49	552	37.1
Nicaragua	64	240	66.4
Panama	59	560	52.4
Paraguay	33	328	43.2
Peru	53	424	40.8
Uruguay	41	300	27.6
Venezuela, R. B. de	68	864	51.9
LAC	41.3	430.5	49.1
OECD	15.3	202.9	47.8

Source: World Bank and IFC 2006.

There is no an equivalent to the transaction tax in Chile, Peru, Ecuador, and El Salvador, and most of the countries that have an equivalent tax apply lower rates than Bolivia (3 percent): Costa Rica (0.3), Nicaragua (1), República Bolivariana de Venezuela (0.8), Colombia (0.97), and Argentina (3). Moreover, the transaction tax hampers commercial relations between firms and incentives imports because it is a cascade tax applied only to local transactions (Coelho et al. 2004). Fiscal constraints, in particular treasury fragility, have made difficult in the medium term to drop the transaction tax or reduce its rate. The VAT has been found to propagate informality along the productive chain in Brazil (Paula and Scheinkman 2006).

Formal firms spend too much time preparing tax payments. A medium-size company requires more time to pay taxes in Bolivia (1,080 hours a year) than in most of the countries in the region because the number of payments is high compared with best practices in the region and each payment requires too much time. While in Bolivia social security contributions and VAT are paid monthly, in Argentina, Brazil, Chile, and Ecuador they are paid only once a year. In addition, the time required by each VAT payment in the countries with monthly payments is below the required time in Bolivia (40 hours): Peru (16), Costa Rica (16), El Salvador (8), Mexico (16), Nicaragua (6.7), and Uruguay (1.2). Therefore, there is some space to reduce the required time to pay taxes, reduce the number of taxes, or make payment more user-friendly.

In this context, small firms choose to remain informal or register themselves in the simplified tax regime despite the disadvantage involved in accessing markets. The fast and cheap simplified tax regime was designed to cover small firms with no accounting books (Box 1.1). However, as is the case of fully informal firms, enterprises registered in the simplified tax regime are disadvantaged by the VAT, because they cannot make use of the fiscal credit generated by the inputs they acquire from formal providers, nor can they generate fiscal credit to their formal clients, limiting the interrelation between formal and informal firms (DECMA 2006). Therefore, reducing tax regulation or improving the design of the simplified tax regime could persuade entrepreneurs in favor to formality.

Labor regulation restrict both firm and labor formality

The flexibility of labor markets is constrained by the heavy regulation on the hiring and firing of workers despite a low minimum wage. Bolivia has overly protective labor regulations dating from 1939 and the government has recently increased the restrictions on labor dismissal in an effort to enhance labor stability (Table 1.6). This legal framework restricts firms' abilities to adjust to economic conditions and makes entrepreneurs more risk averse to hire new workers. Moreover, this regulation makes it difficult to increase *labor* formalization, even if the *firm* has a certain degree of formalization; some firms, in particular the small ones, could register to operate and report taxes, but do not comply with labor laws. In contrast, Bolivia fares well in regard to minimum wage regulations because it is relatively low compared to average wages and hence it has a relatively high level of compliance (World Bank 2005b).

By regional standards, in Bolivia, dismissals are severely constrained, firing costs are high, and vacations are long:

Box 1.1. Most important tax regimes in Bolivia

The general regime is required for all enterprises with total capital above US$3,077 (or Bs. 18,800) and is opened to other firms that do not want to register under the simplified regime. Under the general regime, firms or entrepreneurs face higher registration and recurrent costs than under the simplified regime. The total costs are estimated at around US$63. The main cost (around US$60) comes from the requirement under the general regime that the firms' balance sheet be prepared by a certified accountant and presented within 30 days of registration. If the firm has been incorporated as a society (*Sociedad Anónima or Sociedad de Responsabilidad Limitada*), then a copy of the document of incorporation and a power of attorney to the firm's legal representative may drive the cost to US$210. The recurrent costs include paying the services of an accountant to estimate the monthly value-added tax (VAT) (13 percent), the transaction tax (3 percent), and the income tax payments that the firm needs to pay. The annual cost of accounting can be estimated at around US$450.

The simplified regime is for very small enterprises or firms with less capital. The total cost of registering under the simplified regime can be estimated at around US$3 and takes less than a day to complete. The main difference from the general regime is that the simplified regime imposes no recurrent accounting costs. However, under the general regime, the firm or entrepreneur gets a VAT refund for the taxes paid at the time of purchasing material inputs. The tax refund is not available under the simplified regime. Hence, firms under the simplified regime pay taxes and can issue receipts, but they cannot provide tax returns to their customers (*emission de facturas sin derechos fiscales*).

▨ The difficulty of firing index is at 100, the highest possible ranking, compared with 26.5 for LAC because termination of workers due to redundancy is not authorized while most of the countries in the region have legally authorized it (Annex 1.4). Some countries, including Brazil, Costa Rica, and El Salvador, do not have restrictions, while Chile only requires a notification to authorities.

▨ The difficulty of hiring index is well above the regional average because in Bolivia term contracts can be used only for term tasks while in other countries including Chile, Colombia, Ecuador, and Nicaragua this restriction does not exist. Moreover, while term contracts are limited to three years in Bolivia, other countries such as Colombia, Cost Rica, El Salvador, and Mexico there are no time limits.

▨ In Bolivia a formal employer must pay the equivalent of 100 weeks of salary to dismiss a worker—one of the highest firing costs in the region. Moreover, an employer in Bolivia is required to give a 90-day notice before a redundancy termination, and the penalty for a redundancy dismissal for workers with 20 years of service equals 21 months of wages.

▨ The rigidity of hours index is high mainly because vacations are long in comparison with regional standards: an employee with 20 years of service has 30 days of paid vacation in Bolivia, 20 in Mexico, 18 in Chile, 15 in Colombia, 12 in Costa Rica, and 11 in El Salvador.

Table 1.7. Labor regulation burden in Latin American countries

	Difficulty of Hiring Index	Rigidity of Hours Index	Difficulty of Firing Index	Rigidity of Employment Index*	Nonwage labor cost % of salary	Firing costs weeks of wages
Argentina	44	60	20	41	23	138.7
Bolivia	61	60	100	74	13.7	99.5
Brazil	67	60	0	42	37.3	36.8
Chile	33	20	20	24	3.4	52
Colombia	22	40	20	27	27.6	58.6
Costa Rica	56	40	0	32	26	35.3
Ecuador	44	60	50	51	12.2	135.4
El Salvador	33	40	0	24	8.9	85.7
Mexico	33	40	40	38	23.9	74.3
Nicaragua	11	60	0	24	17	23.8
Panama	78	20	70	56	19.4	44
Paraguay	56	60	60	59	16.5	112.9
Peru	44	60	80	61	9.8	52
Uruguay	33	60	0	31	6.2	31.2
Venezuela, R. B. de	67	60	100	76	15.7	47.3
LAC	34	34.8	26.5	31.7	12.5	59
OECD	27	45.2	27.4	33.3	21.4	31.3

Source: World Bank and IFC 2006.
Note: The rigidity of employment index is the average of difficulty of hiring, rigidity of hours, and difficulty of firing indexes.

The nonwage labor cost is not the most important labor constraint. In Bolivia the nonwage labor cost amounts to 13.7 percent of the worker's wages and includes 10 percent for sickness, maternity, and temporary disability benefits; 1.7 percent for permanent disability and survivor benefits; and 2 percent for housing (World Bank and IFC 2006). This cost is close to regional average (12.5) although some countries, including Chile (3.4), El Salvador (8.9), Peru (9.8), and Uruguay (6.2), have lower nonwage costs.

However, regulation is not identified as a mayor constraint by entrepreneurs because it may be effectively circumvented. The most recent WEF survey reports relative flexibility in wage determination for Bolivia (44 of 125 countries) and in the ease of hiring and firing practice (43 of 125 countries). Moreover, evidence from the ICA 2006 suggests that labor regulations are not a major constraint to the functioning of firms, and all firms regardless of their size share that opinion (chapter 2 covers the impact of regulation on firm's productivity). These results suggest that the Labor Law may effectively be circumvented by businesses due to insufficient enforcement related to labor ministry weakness. Enforcement and labor conflicts resolution are too centralized in this underfunded and stretched ministry. In this context, any effort to improve labor regulation enforcement without a previous reduction of the regulation burden could increase informality, particularly labor informality.

Weak institutions make informality even more attractive

Weak public institutions and low education levels magnify the burden of regulation. Bolivia ranks below the Latin American average in all the institutional indicators calculated by Kaufmann (Figure 1.16), although some progress have been attained in a handful of public institutions, such as the Customs and the Tax Service.

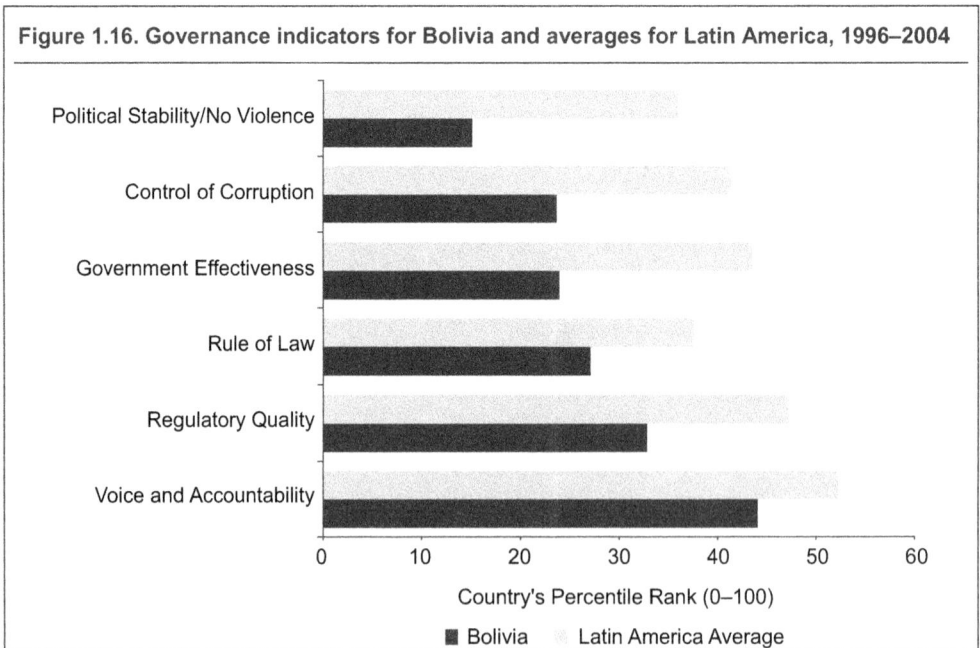

Figure 1.16. Governance indicators for Bolivia and averages for Latin America, 1996–2004

Source: Kaufmann, Kraay, and Mastruzzi 2006.

These weaknesses tend to reduce the government's capacity to apply the law, reducing the penalty risk for informal firms as well as the capacity of public agencies to simplify regulation without creating legal loopholes. Complex regulations enacted by governments that "lack the capability to enforce compliance" encourage informality (Loayza 1996). Additionally, the political instability generated by institutional weakness makes informality more attractive, because informal factor mobility— moving to another market or exiting the market—is easier because of the absence of regulation and control. Moreover, low education levels are probably restraining the creation of formal businesses because poorly educated workers are less able to deal with the complexity of the regulation (*Encuestas y Estudios* 2007). Despite the significant achievements in access to primary and secondary education, educational quality is still very poor. Only 31 percent of students at the sixth year of primary school attain the learning goals in language, and only 44 percent meet the goals in mathematics.

Institutional weaknesses reduce the advantage of formality. According to the World Economic Forum (2006) survey of formal enterprises, political instability, corruption, government instability, and bureaucratic inefficiency are among the most important problems for doing business in Bolivia (Figure 1.17).

Figure 1.17. Most problematic factors for doing business, according to formal entrepreneurs operating in Bolivia

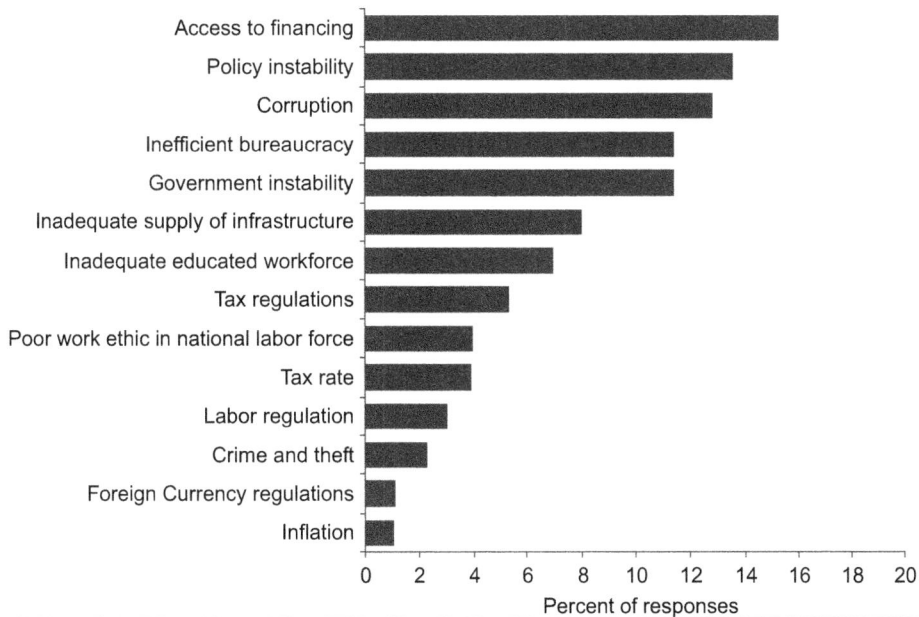

Source: World Economic Forum 2006.

Note: From a list of 14 factors, respondents were asked to select the five most problematic for doing business in the country and to rank them between 1 (most problematic) and 5. The bars in the figure show the responses weighted according to their rankings.

Those factors related with institutional weakness are at least as important as access to finance and more important than low education levels, infrastructure restrictions, and labor regulations. Institutional weakness restrains the government from supplying quality services in critical areas related to the promotion of commercial and productive activities, such as the protection of private property and the provision of an adequate framework for commercial transactions, easy and expeditious access to courts and justice, and protection against corrupt practices (Schneider and Enste 2000). Institutional weakness restrains formality because entrepreneurs perceive that formalization does not guarantee access to high-quality public services.

Corruption is perceived as an important constraint by firms, in particular the smaller ones. Most entrepreneurs perceived that political instability and competition from the informal sector are the mayor constraints to their business (ICA 2006). (Chapter 2 discusses the perceived constraints to productivity using the ICA data). However, corruption is another important constraint affecting mostly small enterprises—two thirds of small firms consider corruption is an important or major obstacle to their functioning, compared to 55 percent of large firms. Bolivia is ranked 88th among 125 countries on business cost of corruption partially because it is ranked 117th and 96th on irregular payments in judicial decisions (see Figure 1.18). Irregular payments in other institutions seem less common—Bolivia is ranked 77th, 69th and 76th on irregular payments in international trade, public utilities, and tax collection respectively. However, paradoxically, few firms declare that the functioning of courts represents a significant obstacle to then, in particular small firms, despite the fact that 90 percent of large firms and 64 percent of small firms use the court system to resolve their payment disputes.

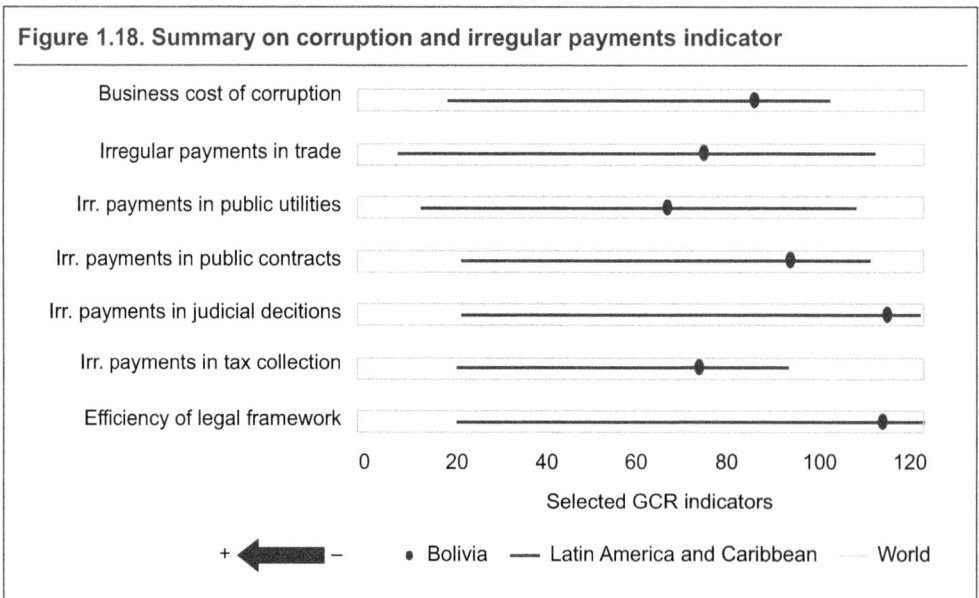

Figure 1.18. Summary on corruption and irregular payments indicator

Source: WEF 2006.

The low quality of public services offered to formal employees encourages labor to turn to informality. A worker may prefer a formal job, at a given wage, if the related nonpecuniary benefits—such as adequate health insurance, labor protection, and pension schemes—were high enough. But formal institutional weaknesses reduce the quality of these benefits, restraining the appeal of formal employment. For example, it is common in Bolivia that formal workers who benefit from a health insurance service opt for a higher-quality service with a private medical supplier. Furthermore, more than 30 percent of workers not registered in any pension fund do not trust the long-term social security system managed by the AFPs and 40 percent do not even know about these funds, according to the 2005 Household Survey. Finally, effective worker protection against employer mistreatment is poor, despite the highly protective labor law (World Bank 2005a). The government has made great efforts to protect workers, but its limited implementation capacity lowers the quality of its services.

Why Should We Care about the Informal Sector?

Informality could be constraining productivity growth

Informal firms tend to have less output per worker. The difference in labor productivity between firms that started up informally and firms that have always operated formally is close to 30 percent in Bolivia, after controlling for firms size, time in the business, sector, and region. This is similar to Mexico and Panama but higher than Argentina, where the productivity gap amounts to less than 20 percent and Uruguay and Colombia, where there is no gap (World Bank 2007). However, this conclusion does not discard that some informal firms could be more dynamic than formals ones. Moreover, the literature underlines that informality may have negative effects on firm productivity, by different channels:

- Informal firms are at a disadvantage in obtaining credit. Even if micro financing is an important option for informal firms, closely following their specific characteristics and requirements, there is still a negative cost spread compared with traditional funding.
- Informal firms have limited access to exports, because of the sizable volumes involved and the additional administrative procedures required that usually demand prior formalization (World Bank and IFC 2006; Ministry of Labor 2006). In this context, less than 2 percent of micro and small firms access an international market, even when their products do not show quality restrictions (Borda and Ramirez 2006). Given the limited interrelations between formal and informal firms, related to the tax issues described above, this restriction is very difficult to overcome.
- In their effort to be undetectable to official control, informal firms are usually very small. This situation hampers their ability to obtain economies of scale, at least in some sectors. This restriction may be less important in the services sector, where there may be less room for economies of scale (Lewis 2004) and where there is a massive participation of informal labor. As a result of their small scale, informal firms can be less motivated to use technological innovations and increase their brand-creating efforts.

⬚ Firms that are insufficiently competitive and in other circumstances would be forced to withdraw from the market can remain active in the informal sector. This outcome, although it behaves as an alternative to a social protection network, slows down the flow of human and capital resources to more dynamic and productive sectors, triggering a low productivity trap (IADB 2003).

⬚ In the absence of formal labor contracts, informal firms usually maintain frail relations with their employees, restraining mutual incentives to increase human capital and hence productivity.

However, there is no clear empirical evidence that informality negatively affects aggregate growth. Loayza et al. (2005) find a negative, although weak, correlation between the level of informality and growth. This relation does not imply any causality relation and looses significance when standard growth determinants are controlled. However, this could be due to the fact that growth determinants can also affect informality and it is not possible to distinguish among their direct effect on growth and those that operate through informality. In any case, the relation among productivity of the formal and informal sector is not being reduced.

Informality erodes formal social protection networks and public services

Informality hinders formal social protection coverage. Although the informal sector creates significant employment opportunities, it leaves informal employees beyond any labor protection, formal social security, and health services. Moreover, informal employees are further at risk because informal activities are often conducted in unsafe workplaces (Chen 2005b). It is worth noting, however, that informal social networks may mitigate, at least partially, the lack of formal services, even if with narrower coverage and services. The low quality associated with formal suppliers makes the alternative informal networks more attractive (Maloney 2003).

Informality usually reduces fiscal revenues, trimming down the supply of public services and eroding legal compliance. Informal firms do not pay taxes, but freely use some of the public services supported by taxation. This free-riding implies that taxpayers ultimately will have to pay more to preserve the supply of public services. The sheer size of the informal sector also dilutes the government's ability to enforce compliance with regulation, because informal firms or workers do not perceive any punitive or limitative action to their activities. This problem is exacerbated by the inefficiency and corruption of some public institutions (Henley et al. 2006).

Informality further erodes public institutions by circumventing formal mechanisms. On one hand, the inefficiency of formal institutions hampers business association arrangements, especially in regard to other partners' misconduct. As a result, entrepreneurs choose not to associate (World Bank 2001). On the other hand, some informal firms may keep their activity at a personal or family level, which hinders their capacity to obtain economies of scale. The opportunity to formalize is also weakened because formality costs are independent of the firm size in each registry stage.[3] As a consequence, 90 percent of blue- and white-collar workers in firms with less than five employees are not registered in a pension fund. Selecting an informal mechanism to overcome the problems that formal institutions do not solve may encompass the business management processes, including the selection of suppliers, employees and financing sources. Such alternative mechanisms are often characterized by their high exclusivity and distortion.

Conclusions

Bolivia's rate of informality is among the highest in Latin America and the trend has been constant in recent years. According to a definition based on worker characteristics and firm size, 77 percent of employment in Bolivia is informal, which is the highest level in the region. Since 1990 informality has fluctuated without a definite trend. Between 1997 and 2002, the annual growth of informality in Bolivia was near 0.5 percent and below most countries in the region.

The informal sector is characterized by its heterogeneity attracting both successful entrepreneurs as well as those disadvantaged in the formal sector. While three quarters of the population without education is informal, only one third of the population with higher education is. Women are strongly represented in the informal sector, 90 percent of them are self-employed. Indigenous people are also strongly represented, with two thirds of self-identified indigenous people who are informal, compared with half of all the nonindigenous.

The big size of the informal sector can be blamed on the heavy burden of regulation, weak institutions, and the lack of clear benefits to formalization. The regulatory burden is among the main causes of informality in Bolivia, because it increases formality costs. However, the weakness of public institutions tends to reduce the benefits of formalization and moderates the costs related with informality: weak public institutions are not able to supply high-quality public services required by formal firms or effectively enforce the law. In this context, firms perceive that the costs of formalization related among others to the regulatory burden are not offset by clear benefits.

The size of the informal sector has negative implications for growth and the provision of public goods. Informality has negative effects on firm productivity, and also negative externalities on social protection coverage, fiscal revenues collection, and the supply of public services.

Annex 1.1. The complexity of defining informality

There is no universal definition of informality, and the availability of information dictates operational definitions allowing measurement and analysis. Informality is usually understood under the dualist, the structuralist, or the legalist approaches. Dualism considers that the informal economy acts as a safety net for the poor because slow economic growth in the formal sector cannot absorb new entrants to the labor market. Structuralism considers that informality is subordinated to the formal sector to reduce costs, with the effect of transferring the informal firms' surplus to the formal sector, due to deliberate actions taken by formal capitalists (Poveda 2003). Legalism sees the informal sector as an entrepreneurial escapism from excessive bureaucracy and red tape (Chen 2005a). Considering this diversity of approaches, it is not surprising that there is no universally accepted definition of informality. Even the use of the term is not unanimous. Expressions like shadow, underground, bazaar, parallel, gray economy, and even murky are applied. Some analysts believe that the search for a universal definition of informality is pointless (Lay 2003). Information restrictions compel the use of operational definitions that permit analysis. These operational definitions are based on characteristics of people or productive units in the sector.

The definitions of informality related to the number of employees, the business registry, or the fulfillment of existing norms in business management are frequently applied in empirical investigations. The first operational definition was based on the number of employees in the productive units. This empirical approach is justified by the strong link between micro enterprises and what is generally understood as informality. Another option to define informality, based on the characteristics of the productive unit and popularized by De Soto (1989), is its formal registry. Similarly, informality can be evaluated by the level of unreported sales for tax purposes, the existence of a formal labor relation (Lay 2003) and if this relation includes some kind of social security, as medical coverage or participation in a formal retirement scheme. However, these definitions are not free from ambiguities. The number of employees is only an approximation for informality: some formal activities, such as professional self-employment, can be defined as informal, and informally managed medium enterprises can be defined as formal. In addition, the registry of a firm has different stages resulting in several degrees of formality. Numerous operational definitions can be applied to evaluate different informality dimensions. Moreover, these definitions are not fully coherent among themselves (Henley et al. 2006).

These operational definitions can be classified in different ways. According to Gasparini and Tornarolli (2007), labor informality definitions can be grouped into two categories: the "productive" definitions consider that informal jobs are less productive, and the "legalist" definitions focus on the absence of formal social protection. This classification is not exhaustive because firms' informality is not considered. Additionally, operative informality definitions can group informality by the status of individuals or by the characteristics of the employer (Henley et al. 2006). Informality definitions based on individual status include workers who are self-employed, who are domestic employees, who are without a formal labor relation with their employer, or who do not benefit from a social security program. Informality definitions related to the characteristics of the employer include firms that are small, that are not registered, or that have undeclared sales.

This document uses a set of informality definitions to try to capture the various dimensions of this phenomenon, considering the available information. For example, to evaluate the sociodemographic characteristics of informal workers, definitions based on the size of the productive unit, the extent of social security system coverage, and the type of employment will be used to take advantage of the information provided by household surveys. Figure 1.A.1.1 shows a regional comparison on informality under different definitions, estimated using household surveys. Additionally, subsequent chapters will use information obtained from the survey prepared for this document to identify informal firms according to their level of official registration and evaluate their productivity constraints. In Bolivia, official registration as a formal business can be accomplished through six different steps: (i) getting a tax identification number (NIT) from the tax service; (ii) registering with FundEmpresa; (iii) obtaining a municipal license; (iv) registering with the national health insurance; (v) registering with pension funds (also known as AFPs—*Administradoras de Fondos de Pensiones*); and (vi) registering with the Labor Ministry (Ministry of Labor 2006).

The chapter uses mostly two definitions of informality: the productive and the legalistic definitions. This chapter uses the Household Survey 2005, taking advantage of the informality module included in this survey. It is focused on urban areas because rural areas are largely dominated by the agrarian economy with little formal labor relations (Landa et al. 2007); the Household Survey 2005 informality module was not applied in rural areas. Its analysis is limited to the employed population who is at least 10 years old, following national practices. Based on this information two informality definitions are used in this chapter:

- *A productive definition based on labor categories and size of firms.* Under this definition, an individual who belongs to the following categories is considered informal: (i) informal salaried, including blue- and white-collar workers and remunerated employers working in private establishments with less than five partners; and (ii) informal nonsalaried including unremunerated employees and cooperative workers in establishments with less than five people, as well as the self-employed and family workers. Following national practices, domestic employees are considered as a separated category in the labor market. The formal sector considers the following categories: (i) all public employees, in an effort to isolate the effect of public employment on private labor markets; (ii) formal salaried, including blue- and white-collar workers, as well as remunerated employees in private establishments with more than four partners; and (iii) formal nonsalaried, including unremunerated employees and cooperative workers in establishments with more than five people.
- *A legalistic definition.* Under this definition a worker not affiliated to a pension plan is informal. Both formal and informal sectors were divided into salaried and nonsalaried workers: (i) salaried including blue- and white-collar workers, remunerated employers and domestic employees; (ii) nonsalaried including unremunerated employees, cooperatives and family workers.

Figure 1.A.1.1. Selected indicators of informality in Latin America

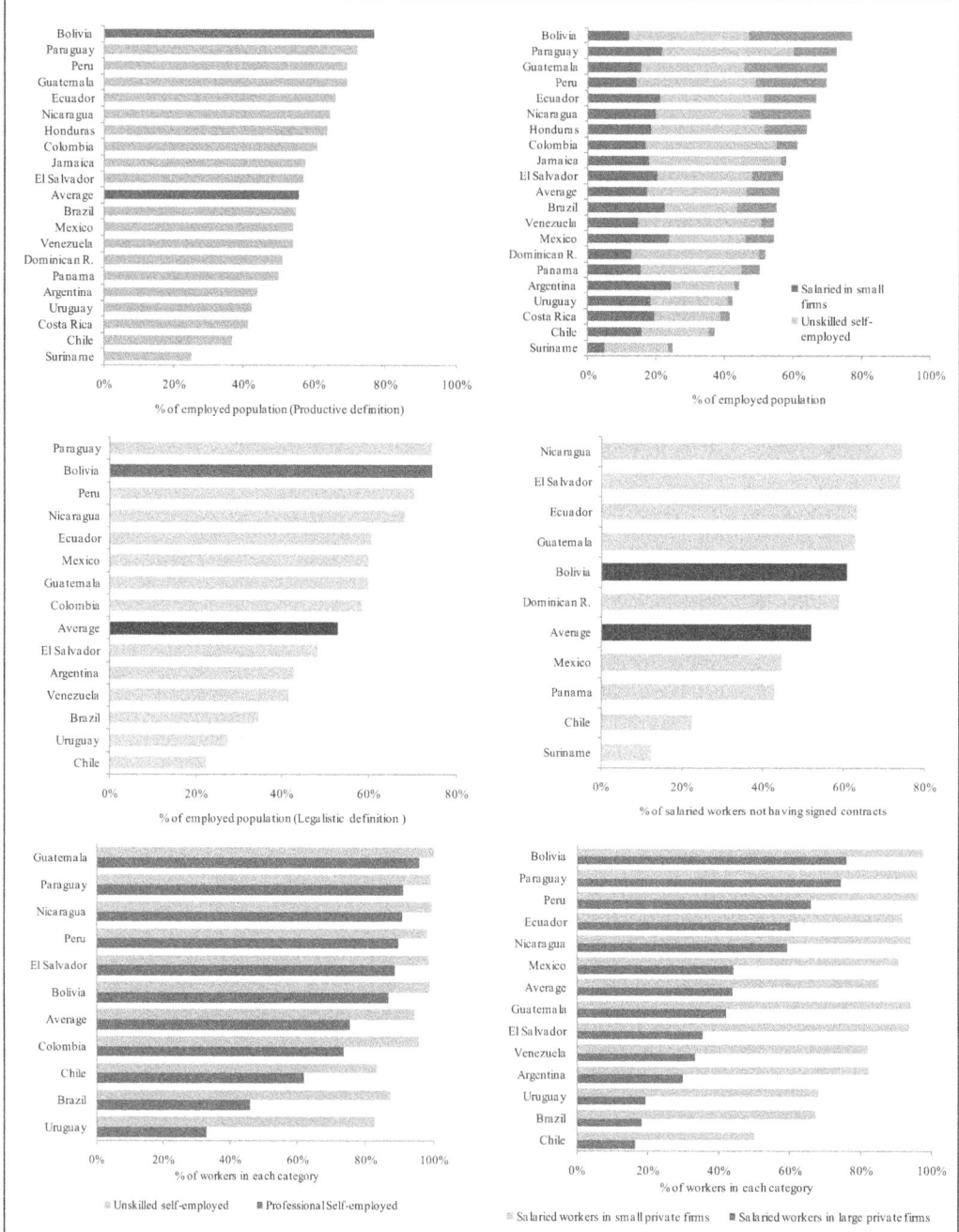

Source: Gasparini and Tornarolli 2007.

Note: The productive definition includes unskilled self-employed, paid employees working in micro firms and nonsalaried workers, but it does not include employers. Under the legalistic definition, a salaried worker is considered informal if he does not have the right to a pension, linked to his employment, when retired. The MECOVI 2002 was used for Bolivia.

Figure 1.A.1.2. Methods to measure the size of the informal sector

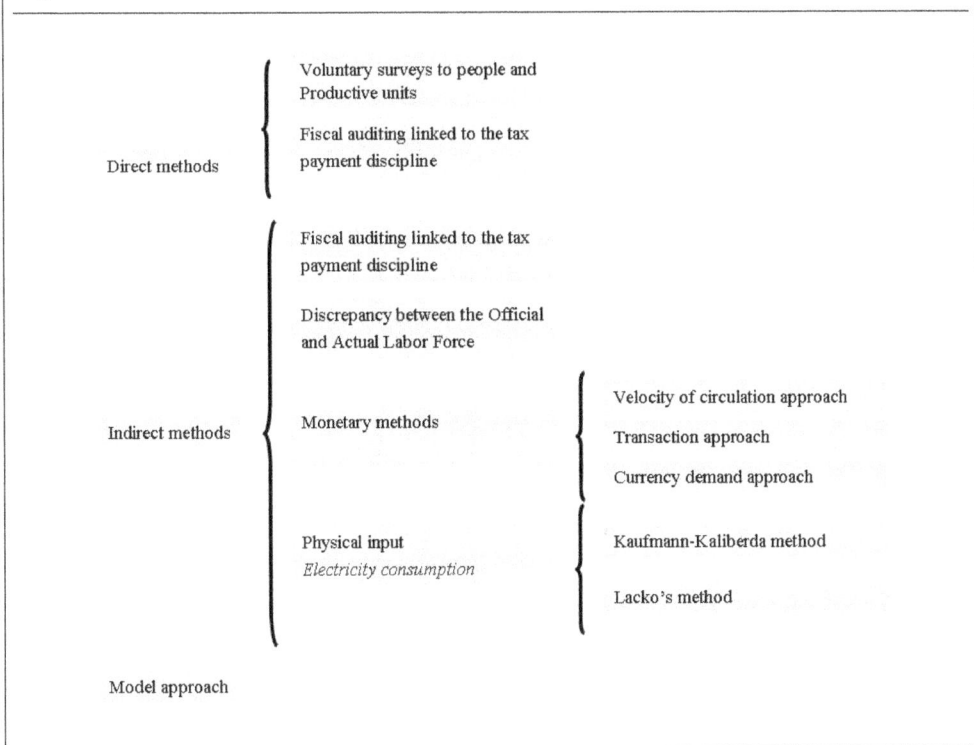

Direct methods
- Voluntary surveys to people and Productive units
- Fiscal auditing linked to the tax payment discipline

Indirect methods
- Fiscal auditing linked to the tax payment discipline
- Discrepancy between the Official and Actual Labor Force
- Monetary methods
  - Velocity of circulation approach
  - Transaction approach
  - Currency demand approach
- Physical input *Electricity consumption*
  - Kaufmann-Kaliberda method
  - Lacko's method

Model approach

Source: Schneider 2002; Schneider y Enste 2000.

Those definitions are broadly used in the chapter to evaluate the characteristics of informal workers. However, alternative definitions are also used to take advantage of previous works on informality and the information of other surveys and databases.

Additionally, there are several methods to estimate the value-added of informal sector. The operational definitions cannot measure the value-added generated in the informal sector. Nor can this information be obtained from the national accounts, where the informal sector is not fully and explicitly identified. To overcome these restrictions, there are a variety of methods to measure informal production (Annex Figure 1.A.2), considering data availability. These methods are grouped as direct, indirect, and model approaches.

- Direct approaches use information obtained by voluntary surveys or by fiscal auditing programs, such as tax audit. In voluntary surveys, detailed information can be obtained but the importance of informality in monetary terms depends on the willingness of respondents to disclose this information. Tax auditing measures undeclared income, helping to calculate the size of informality, but the sample may be biased (tax samples are usually not random) and incomplete (fully informal sectors may not be considered).

■   Indirect or indicator approaches use economic indicators as proxies for the evolution of informality over time, comparing these indicators with other observable variables concerning the formal sector. For example, total labor data from surveys or census may be compared with formal labor data from other sources, allowing the estimation of informal labor as a residual. The same principle can be applied to calculate the value added by the informal sector.

■   The model approach considers multiple causes to and multiple indicators of informality and its evolution over time. Using the statistical theory of unobserved variables—in this case, informality—and a set of structural equations that link causes and indicators with the unobserved variable, it is possible to estimate the size of the informal sector.

Annex 1.2. Sociodemographic characteristics of formal and informal workers under the productive definition, 2005

	Total	Formal					Informal and Domestic sector				
		Total	Public	Private			Total	Informal sector			Domestic
				Total	Salaried	Nonsalaried		Total	Salaried	Nonsalaried	
Distribution											
	100.0	37.1	9.8	27.2	24.7	2.5	62.9	59.1	12.6	46.6	3.8
Male	100.0	44.5	9.0	35.5	32.0	3.5	55.5	55.4	16.7	38.7	0.1
Female	100.0	27.5	10.9	16.6	15.3	1.3	72.5	63.9	7.3	56.7	8.5
Sex											
Male	56.3	67.6	51.6	73.3	72.9	77.4	49.7	52.8	74.8	46.8	2.2
Female	43.7	32.4	48.4	26.7	27.1	22.6	50.3	47.2	25.2	53.2	97.8
Age group											
15–24	21.9	21.1	7.8	25.8	27.8	6.1	22.4	20.6	30.2	18.1	49.2
25–34	26.4	31.5	29.0	32.4	33.2	24.4	23.3	23.6	34.5	20.6	19.6
35–44	22.7	21.5	23.7	20.7	19.9	29.0	23.4	23.8	20.5	24.7	17.0
45–54	16.9	17.8	29.3	13.7	12.2	28.0	16.3	16.7	10.6	18.4	10.0
55–64	8.7	6.7	9.3	5.8	5.6	8.5	9.9	10.4	3.1	12.4	2.1
65 and more	3.4	1.3	0.3	0.5	1.2	4.2	4.7	4.8	1.1	5.8	2.1
Average age	36.7	35.5	40.1	33.8	33.1	41.1	37.3	37.9	31.6	39.5	29.2
Education											
None	4.0	2.3	2.6	2.1	1.5	8.1	5.0	4.9	1.9	5.7	7.1
Incomplete primary	30.3	17.8	6.1	21.9	21.4	26.9	37.6	37.2	27.7	39.8	43.6
Completed primary	5.7	3.5	1.6	4.2	3.9	8.2	7.0	7.0	7.8	6.8	8.0
Incomplete secondary	14.8	12.1	4.3	14.9	14.8	15.1	16.4	16.0	20.2	14.9	21.8
Completed secondary	19.3	19.3	11.7	22.0	22.7	15.6	19.4	19.6	25.2	18.1	15.4
Tertiary	25.4	44.6	73.3	34.3	35.3	24.9	14.1	14.8	15.8	14.5	3.3
Other	0.5	0.4	0.3	0.5	0.4	1.1	0.5	0.5	1.5	0.3	0.7
Years of education	9.6	11.8	14.2	10.9	11.1	9.5	8.4	8.5	9.4	8.2	7.0
Indigenous											
No indigenous (self-identification)	51.3	60.8	55.7	62.7	64.4	45.9	45.7	45.5	53.4	43.3	49.1
Indigenous (self-identification)	48.7	39.2	44.3	37.3	35.6	54.1	54.3	54.5	46.6	56.7	50.9
No indigenous (language)	75.7	84.7	83.9	85.0	86.8	67.4	70.5	70.3	77.9	68.2	73.3
Indigenous (language)	24.3	15.3	16.1	15.0	13.2	32.6	29.5	29.7	22.1	31.8	26.7
Economic sector											
Primary	8.5	8.7	0.8	11.5	7.3	52.9	8.4	9.0	3.8	10.4	0.0
Secondary	26.4	32.9	8.1	41.9	43.3	27.6	22.5	24.0	31.2	22.1	0.0
Tertiary	65.1	58.4	91.0	46.6	49.4	19.6	69.0	67.0	65.0	67.6	100.0
Migration											
No migrant	92.6	92.2	94.0	91.5	91.8	88.6	92.8	92.8	90.7	93.4	92.4
Migrant	6.6	6.7	5.4	7.1	6.9	9.2	6.5	6.5	8.4	6.0	7.1
Migrant	0.9	1.2	0.6	1.4	1.3	2.2	0.7	0.7	0.9	0.6	0.5
Family information											
Single	27.5	29.7	25.8	31.0	33.3	8.3	26.3	24.3	36.5	21.0	56.8
Married	64.1	63.1	67.3	61.5	59.3	83.3	64.8	66.8	56.9	69.5	32.9
Divorced	8.3	7.3	6.9	7.4	7.3	8.4	9.0	8.9	6.6	9.5	10.3
Number of child	1.6	1.5	1.7	1.5	1.4	2.3	1.7	1.7	1.5	1.8	1.2
Average firm side	109.4	278.9	729.4	116.8	92.7	353.9	3.2	3.2	2.7	3.3	..
Memo items											
Hours of work per day	48.2	47.4	37.1	51.1	50.4	58.7	48.7	48.5	51.6	47.6	52.7
Average labor income	1272.4	1981.9	2182.8	1909.6	1792.1	3066.0	854.8	872.0	817.0	886.8	588.6
Gini (Labor income)	58.0	51.6	44.9	53.7	53.1	50.8	58.2	59.2	37.7	63.6	28.3
Poverty	42.4	30.3	20.4	33.8	34.4	28.6	49.7	49.8	53.7	48.7	47.2

Source: EDH 2005.

Note: The productive definition of informality includes self-employed, family workers as well as employees and employers working in private establishments with less than five people.

Annex 1.3. Sociodemographic characteristics of formal and informal workers under the legalistic definition, 2005

	Total	Formal			Informal		
		Total	Salaried	Nonsalaried	Total	Salaried	Nonsalaried
Distribution	100.0	19.4	16.6	2.7	80.6	34.3	46.4
Male	100.0	21.3	17.5	3.7	78.7	40.3	38.5
Female	100.0	16.9	15.5	1.4	83.1	26.5	56.6
Sex							
Male	56.3	61.8	59.3	76.9	55.0	66.2	46.7
Female	43.7	38.2	40.7	23.1	45.0	33.8	53.3
Age group							
15-24	21.9	10.7	11.4	6.4	24.6	33.3	18.1
25-34	26.4	30.2	31.8	20.2	25.4	31.6	20.9
35-44	22.7	23.1	24.0	17.3	22.6	18.9	25.4
45-54	16.9	22.9	23.6	18.8	15.4	10.7	18.9
55-64	8.7	10.0	7.7	23.7	8.4	4.3	11.5
65 and more	3.4	3.1	1.4	13.7	3.5	1.1	5.3
Average age	36.7	39.7	38.6	47.0	35.9	31.5	39.2
Education							
None	4.0	1.6	0.6	8.2	4.6	3.1	5.7
Incomplete primary	30.3	9.2	6.4	26.5	35.3	29.1	39.9
Completed primary	5.7	3.0	1.9	9.9	6.4	6.1	6.6
Incomplete secondary	14.8	7.2	6.3	12.6	16.6	18.7	15.1
Completed secondary	19.3	14.8	15.4	11.3	20.4	23.2	18.4
Tertiary	25.4	63.5	68.7	31.5	16.2	19.2	14.0
Other	0.5	0.6	0.7	0.0	0.5	0.7	0.3
Years of education	9.6	13.6	14.2	9.7	8.7	9.4	8.2
Indigenous							
No indigenous (self-identification)	51.3	59.8	63.6	36.4	49.3	56.6	43.8
Indigenous (self-identification)	48.7	40.2	36.4	63.6	50.7	43.4	56.2
No indigenous (language)	75.7	86.5	89.6	67.8	73.1	79.8	68.2
Indigenous (language)	24.3	13.5	10.4	32.2	26.9	20.2	31.8
Economic sector							
Primary	8.5	7.6	3.4	32.7	8.7	5.2	11.3
Secondary	26.4	18.8	20.2	10.0	28.2	35.2	23.1
Tertiary	65.1	73.7	76.4	57.3	63.0	59.6	65.6
Migration							
No migrant	92.6	93.3	92.9	95.7	92.4	91.6	93.0
Migrant	6.6	6.2	6.6	4.3	6.6	7.2	6.2
Migrant	0.9	0.5	0.5	0.0	1.0	1.2	0.8
Family information							
Single	27.5	22.3	25.4	3.8	28.8	38.8	21.3
Married	64.1	68.3	65.9	82.8	63.1	54.6	69.5
Divorced	8.3	9.4	8.8	13.3	8.1	6.6	9.2
Number of child	1.6	1.6	1.5	2.0	1.6	1.4	1.8
Firm side							
1-4	57.1	12.7	3.4	69.6	67.8	35.9	91.4
5-19	18.1	19.3	21.7	4.3	17.9	32.2	7.2
20-49	8.4	23.8	27.7	0.0	4.7	10.6	0.4
50-99	4.1	11.1	12.9	0.0	2.4	5.2	0.4
100 and more	12.2	33.1	34.3	26.1	7.2	16.1	0.7
Average firm side	109.4	465.0	500.8	247.8	20.5	39.5	8.0
Memo items							
Hours of work per day	48.2	44.6	43.4	52.5	49.1	50.7	47.9
Average labor income	1272.4	2651.1	2801.1	1731.7	941.4	922.4	955.4
Gini (Labor income)	127239.1	265105.7	280105.3	173170.8	94136.2	92237.1	95540.1
Poverty	42.4	17.2	15.7	26.4	48.5	48.0	48.9

Source: EDH 2005.

Note: The legalistic definition of informality includes those with no affiliation to a pension system.

Notes

[1] This does not include the Bonosol benefit, which is an annual transfer to all people over 65 years.

[2] In a similar way, Canavire and Landa (2006) find that educated workers, less related with informality, have greater unemployment duration, probably due to their higher reserve wage.

[3] This cost is affected by the legal status that the firm is applying to (limited liability companies, one-person companies, and corporations, for example), but once the firm's legal status is chosen, the cost to formalize is independent of its scale (Labor Ministry 2006).

Annex 1.4. Detailed information on labor regulation in Latin American countries

		Argentina	Bolivia	Brazil	Chile	Colombia	Costa Rica	Ecuador	El Salvador	Mexico	Nicaragua	Panama	Paraguay	Peru	Uruguay	Venezuela
Difficulty of Hiring a new worker	Can term contracts be used only for term tasks?	Yes	Yes	Yes	No	No	Yes	No	Yes	Yes	No	Yes	Yes	Yes	Yes	Yes
	What is the maximum duration of term contracts? (in months)	60	36	24	24	No Limit	No Limit	24	No Limit	No Limit	No Limit	12	No Limit	60	No Limit	24
	What is the ratio of mandated minimum wage to the average value added per worker?	0.36	0.38	0.24	0.21	0.52	0.58	0.34	0.16	0.1	0.47	0.45	0.56	0.43	0.17	0.21
Rigidity on working hours	Can the workweek extend to 50 hours (including overtime) for 2 months per year?	Yes	Yes	Yes	Yes	Yes	Yes	Yes	Yes	Yes	Yes	Yes	Yes	Yes	Yes	Yes
	What is the maximum number of working days per week?	6	6	6	6	6	6	5	6	6	6	6	6	6	6	6
	Are there restrictions on night work?	Yes	Yes	Yes	No	Yes	Yes	Yes	Yes	Yes	Yes	No	Yes	Yes	Yes	Yes
	Are there restrictions on "weekly holiday" work?	Yes	Yes	Yes	Yes	Yes	Yes	Yes	Yes	Yes	Yes	No	Yes	Yes	Yes	Yes
	What is the paid annual vacation (in working days) for an employee with 20 years of service?	24	30	30	18	15	12	15	11	20	30	22	30	22	25	30
Difficulty to dismiss a redundant worker	Is the termination of workers due to redundancy legally authorized?	Yes	No	Yes	Yes	Yes	Yes	Yes	Yes	Yes	Yes	Yes	Yes	Yes	Yes	No
	Must the employer notify a third party before terminating one redundant worker?	Yes	—	No	Yes	No	No	No	No	No	No	Yes	Yes	Yes	No	—
	Does the employer need the approval of a third party to terminate one redundant worker?	No	—	No	No	No	No	No	No	No	No	Yes	Yes	Yes	No	—
	Must the employer notify a third party before terminating a group of redundant workers?	Yes	—	No	Yes	Yes	No	Yes	No	Yes	No	Yes	Yes	Yes	No	—
	Does the employer need the approval of a third party to terminate a group of redundant workers?	No	—	No	No	Yes	No	Yes	No	Yes	No	Yes	Yes	Yes	No	—

	Argentina	Bolivia	Brazil	Chile	Colombia	Costa Rica	Ecuador	El Salvador	Mexico	Nicaragua	Panama	Paraguay	Peru	Uruguay	Venezuela
Must the employer consider reassignment or retraining options before redundancy termination?	No	—	No	No	No	No	Yes	No	No	No	No	No	Yes	No	—
Are there priority rules applying to redundancies?	No	—	No	No	No	No	Yes	No	Yes	No	Yes	No	Yes	No	—
Are there priority rules applying to re-employment?	No	—	No	No	No	No	Yes	No	Yes	No	Yes	Yes	Yes	No	—
What is the notice period for redundancy dismissal after 20 years of continuous employment? (weeks of salary)	8.7	12.9	4.3	4.3	0	4.3	4.3	0	0	2.1	0	12.9	0	0	13
What is severance pay for redundancy dismissal after 20 years of employment? (months of salary)	30	0	6	11	13.5	7.2	30.3	19.8	17.2	5	10.2	23.1	12	7.2	7.9
What is legally mandated penalty for redundancy dismissal? (weeks of salary)	0	86.6	6.5	0	0	0	0	0	0	0	0	0	0	0	0
Firing costs (weeks of wages)	138.7	99.5	36.8	52	58.6	35.3	135.4	85.7	74.3	23.8	44	112.9	52	31.2	47.3

Firing costs (weeks of wages)

Source: World Bank and IFC 2006.

44

CHAPTER 2

The Productivity of
Micro and Small Firms

The first chapter established that the big size of the informal sector could be blamed on the heavy burden of regulation, weak institutions, and the lack of clear benefits to formalization. Those factors were also found to limit the productivity of firms as well as productivity growth. This chapter shifts the focus to the firm as a unit of analysis and investigates the constraints to higher productivity for micro and small firms.

Most micro and small firms in Bolivia are informal, hence raising their productivity and the formalization is critical for promoting economic growth. This chapter investigates a range of constraints that currently limit the productivity of Bolivia's micro and small firms, focusing first on inputs (financial, physical, and human capital) and production (technology and competition) and then on the operational, regulatory, and institutional environment (infrastructure, labor, trade and customs regulations, access to courts, and corruption). The qualitative analysis presented here is based on a dozen focus group interviews with micro and small firms selected from six sectors and four geographic areas to broadly represent the active population employed in the informal sector (Box 2.1). These discussions are complemented with an analysis of the operational, regulatory, and institutional framework for small firms based on the 2006 Investment Climate Assessment (ICA) survey for Bolivia, and data from the World Bank micro firm survey conducted for this study.

Why Does Productivity Matter for Micro and Small Firms?

The production level of micro and small firms, most of which are informal, is constrained by low access to productive inputs, even though returns to capital are highest for the smallest firms. Small firms and informal firms are more constrained in accessing productive inputs than larger firms. There is evidence that many small firms are operating below their efficient scale of production. Indeed, based on data from the Mexican National Survey of Micro Enterprises (ENAMIN), McKenzie and Woodruff (2006) show that returns to capital for the smallest firms (capital stocks less than US$200) were 15 percent per month compared with 3 percent per month for the biggest firms (capital stock above US$1,000). This suggests decreasing returns to capital as capital stock increases.

Box 2.1. The focus group methodology

To identify the constraints to higher productivity and formalization perceived by entrepreneurs and workers in Bolivia's large informal sector, this study conducted 12 focus group interviews in El Alto, La Paz, Cochabamba, and Santa Cruz with representatives from firms in six sectors: grocery stores, restaurants and food sales, clothing manufacturing from wool and cloth, clothing manufacturing from llama and alpaca (camelid) wool, passenger and cargo transport, and wood furniture manufacturing. In each of the six sectors, two homogeneous groups of six to eight informal firms were interviewed. The firms were divided by size, with micro firms of less than 5 workers and small firms of 5–20 workers each discussing their perceptions separately.

The selection process

The selection of the six sectors was made to balance representativeness of the active population employed in the informal sector. Firms were chosen to ensure participation from a diversity of industries, from both formal and informal sectors, and from urban and rural areas. The selection therefore includes four of the top five industries for urban informality. Two of the additional sectors surveyed were wood and camelids because: (i) they are linked to the agriculture sector (representing most of rural informality), (ii) they allow for surveys in both urban and rural areas, and (iii) they engage in some export activity. In addition, (iv) they are among the priority sectors for strategic public investment (*complejos productivos*). [a]

The merits and limitations of analyzing firms' perceptions

In addition to the focus group interviews, we use data from the 2006 Investment Climate Assessment (ICA) for Bolivia, as well as our own 2007 micro-enterprise surveys of formal and informal firms. We chose to analyze qualitative data from the three sources to get a broad view of why firms entered their line of business, what type of constraints they face, and what can be done to alleviate the constraints. The sample interviewed is not statistically representative in the focus groups, but is representative for the ICA and the firms' survey. However, the focus group methodology uncovers new evidence about perceptions and helps to reveal the reasons behind firms' behavior.

The main limitations of using data based on firms' perception of the constraints they face (as in the ICA or the micro survey) are related first to issues related to each individual firm's relative optimism or pessimism regarding its environment. Second, each firm may understand each question differently and then treat it differently, inducing a potential excessive heterogeneity in response. Third, there is a reverse causality between the firms' own characteristics with regard to productivity and formality and what firms perceive as constraints—meaning, for example, that more productive firms tend to perceive fewer constraints. Finally, the data do not always reflect the expected strong correlation between constraints and the consequences of those constraints for firms. For instance, there should be a high correlation between firms that complain about corruption and how much or how often they have to pay bribes. All these limitations can be simply checked for in the data and addressed.

The main advantage of perception data is that people make decisions based on their perception of the opportunities and constraints faced. Furthermore, the data allow us to know how each constraint affects each firm through the impact on its productivity. Hence, the perception of the constraint is directly linked to a practical implication for productivity rather than a vague statement. In the light of these merits and limitations, comparative analysis of the constraints faced by informal versus formal firms, small versus micro firms, or firms in one sector versus those in another, for example, should yield better understanding of productivity and formalization issues.

Note: a. The consulting firm Encuestas y Estudios conducted the focus group interviews in February 2007. The firm directly extended invitations to a sample of firms that met the specifications required. See Encuestas y Estudios (2007). The sectors coverage is the same as for the micro study in Chapter 3; more on the choice of the sector can be found in that chapter.

The high returns to capital at very low levels of capital stock for very small firms suggest that incentives to increase their access to credit can help them exploit those returns of scale. There is no minimum investment threshold below which returns to capital are so low that self-employment is discouraged. Hence, there are no capital-related barriers to entering self-employment, provided that firms get access to credit. Furthermore, randomized experiments have shown that firms which report that access to finance is a serious constraint to their productivity also tend to have higher return to capital (McKenzie Woodruff 2007).

The low productivity of the informal sector in Bolivia has negative implications for growth, employment, and the financing of public goods. Although it functions outside the formal economy and free-rides on the direct provision of public goods, Bolivia's large informal sector generates a significant amount of economic activity and government revenue through consumption of goods and payment of value-added taxes (between 13 to 16 percent of the price of the good). Observers predict that the informal sector should shrink as the rest of the economy becomes more productive and draws more workers in, as has occurred in the development process of developed countries (Maloney 2004; Maloney and Levenson 1998).

There is a reverse causality between low productivity and high informality, which may trap informal firms in less productive activities. Informal firms tend to have low productivity because they are not being able to access production factors (financial and human capital) to produce more and more efficiently. In addition, some firms maintain a low scale of operations to avoid being visible to enforcement. The small scale of informal operations traps labor and otherwise productive resources in low-productivity activities. A large informal sector thus implies a low level of productivity for the economy as a whole, and low productivity will push firms toward the informal sector.

The low employment growth rate observed among micro firms suggests that most of them will reach a very small size at their steady state. The high prevalence of small informal firms does not mean that there are high external barriers to growth, because the size distribution of firms may be determined by the underlying distribution of entrepreneurial ability and the costs of operation at different sizes (Lucas 1978; World Bank 2007, chapter 5). Evidence from the World Bank 2007 (chapter 6) suggests that informality is due to a large extent to a prevalence of very small unproductive firms. For informality to decrease, the general levels of productivity would need to rise.

A similar argument suggests that there are many unproductive small firms because formal productivity is low, so the opportunity costs of opening one's own business are low. There is evidence of very low productivity growth in Bolivia (0.2 percent from 1993 to 2000) (Loayza 2004; World Bank 2005b). The low productivity of the formal sector makes it harder for the formal sector to expand and take over most of the informal sector's labor. The low level of productivity in the formal economy is due to many factors, including the current investment climate, which is not conducive to higher productivity. As a consequence, some firms choose to work in the informal sector because it is more attractive for the flexibility it allows and/or for their level of production. However, as firms become more productive, formality gradually becomes more attractive. Increasing the size and productivity of the formal sector may be a good option to decrease the attractiveness of the informal sector for workers in the long run.

The informal sector impedes job reallocation, which accounts for an important part of productivity gains. Productivity gains arise from the technological and managerial improvements at the firm level, the exit of less productive firms, and the movement of employment from less productive firms to more productive firms. The job reallocation process contributes to 15 percent to 50 percent of aggregate productivity growth in Latin America (IDB 2003, cited in Bolivia Poverty Assessment World Bank 2005a). However, when there is an informal sector, formal firms may elect to become informal instead of exiting. Once they are in the informal sector, workers often have a hard time leaving, because informal firms tend to remain small and have a high rate of mortality. Data from Mexico show a high rate of exit among small firms in their first few years (Maloney and Levenson 1998).

The high level of informality associated with lower productivity has strong poverty implications. Informal labor reports higher incidence of poverty than formal labor. A reported 65 percent of the active urban population works in the informal sector, of which 50 percent are poor; among formal employees, only 34 percent are poor ("El Sector informal en los Países Andinos," 2002, cited in Bolivia Poverty Assessment World Bank 2005a). The poverty rate differential between formal and informal worker is partially due to earnings and education differentials: hourly earnings are reportedly 70 to 90 percent higher in the formal sector than for self-employed or salaried workers in the informal sector. However, earnings differentials do not capture the many perquisites that the informal sector offers, such as being your own boss, working from home, and being able to care for children and elders.

The ease of entry and exit in the informal sector makes it a natural safety net for workers. The informal sector allows workers who have lost their jobs to earn some income; it allows business owners more flexibility to modulate their activity depending on the needs of their households (Cunningham and Ramos 2002). As such, it constitutes an important safety net for workers in the formal sector.

The analysis of the focus group interviews suggests that micro and small firms do not always understand the meaning of informality nor the costs and benefits related to informality. For the majority of the members of our focus groups, formality means *dar facturas* or providing formal receipts. This is related to paying taxes, as firms need to be registered with the tax authorities to issue those receipts (Box 2.2). For others, formality means being registered at the municipal level and paying a *patente*[1] or a *sentaje*,[2] or getting a municipal license to operate. The most extreme definition of formalization comes from the transport sector, where it amounts to being affiliated with a union or a business association. For those firms and other micro and small firms, formality does not mean having a NIT, paying taxes, being registered with FundEmpresa (which many had never even heard of), or being registered with the Labor Ministry, Social Security, or the *Caja de Salud* as required by the law (Encuestas y Estudios 2007).

Box 2.2. Incentives for formality from the focus groups

Most micro and small firms are informal by all criteria. The few firms that have some degree of formality (mainly having a tax number) are found in exporting sectors: camelid-derived products and wood manufacturing. As with other sectors, size matters, as almost all the bigger micro and small firms had a tax number, were registered at the municipal level and with FundEmpresa, and some also belonged to a Chamber of Commerce or an exporting association. Those firms reported that the main benefit of formality was to enable them to export, as they could get the necessary documents. Because the benefits of exporting were greater than the costs of complying with the formalization process, those firms did formalize. Firms that have a tax number reported that issuing receipts also enabled them to expand their client base. However, they complained that issuing receipts attracted the attention of tax inspectors. Only the biggest firms of the sample would offer to provide receipts to their clients, which suggests that the benefits of formality increased with the size of the firm and its level of production.

In other sectors, formalization is perceived as an additional cost of doing business and a reduction in earnings. The case of transport is interesting in that firms thought of formality as being affiliated with a union or a business association. [a] The benefits of "formalization" as they define it encompass getting a monopoly on certain routes, getting protection from crime and violence (especially in cities such as Santa Cruz), getting access to credit through the union or business association, getting timely and cheaper access to vehicles parts through the union, and avoiding paying fines and taxes using the "influence" of the union. "Informal" firms in that sector, those not affiliated to any union or association, consider that the economic and political costs of affiliation are greater that the cited benefits. This case illustrates well the fact that micro and small firms behave like all other rational firms or that formalization is a normal good in firms' production process (Maloney 2004, 2006). They "view" formalization as a tradeoff between benefits and costs. However, the costs seem overwhelmingly greater than the benefits.

Note: a. More than a decade ago, formalization in transport included affiliation with a union. This has not been the case for many years, but the firms in the sector still consider affiliation the main formalization channel.

The lack of information on informality may have several explanations. Enforcement from tax authorities for micro and small firms seems to be pretty lax and concentrated around high-activity periods like holidays and urban locations close to the tax office. However, the municipalities are very efficient at enforcing registration, which also spreads information. The registry of firms FundEmpresa has not reached out to most micro and small firms even in the urban areas of the central axis (La Paz, El Alto, Cochabamba, and Santa Cruz). Different registries are not working together to share the same information. For instance, the municipal registry may not require a tax number or a registration to FundEmpresa.

What Is Constraining the Productivity of Micro and Small Firms?

Productivity gains can be defined as the increase in production that exceeds the increase in production factors (labor-hours worked or capital-units of capital). This section examines an array of factors that are constraining productivity gains in Bolivia. The analysis evaluates the effect of the scale of operation on the productivity of micro and small firms in the formal and informal sectors. We draw upon data from the World Bank micro-enterprise survey (2007) collected for this study and the Investment Climate Assessment (ICA) data (2006) to contrast the constraints identified by micro and small firms with those affecting medium and large firms. We then use the focus group materials to discuss the constraints posed by limited access to inputs (financial capital, physical capital, labor and human capital, as well as access to raw materials and a supply chain of component parts). The analysis also addresses specific obstacles in the production function related to technology, quality, and competition. Section 3 then examines the impact of the institutional and regulatory environment on productivity.

Scale of operation

For micro firms, informality poses fewer constraints on productivity than formality. Informal micro firms' top five constraints to growth are crime, corruption, macro instability, cost of credit, and political instability. Formal micro firms' top five constraints are crime, customs regulations, corruption, informal competition, and macro instability. Informality shields the informal micro firms from costs related to formality, such as costly customs and trade regulation, taxes, and labor regulations. Nonetheless, access to equipment and credit is smaller for informal micro firms, and they are more exposed to corruption. Both types of firms report the same constraints to productivity from crime and informal competition (Figure 2.1).

Figure 2.1. Constraints on higher productivity for micro firms, by formality

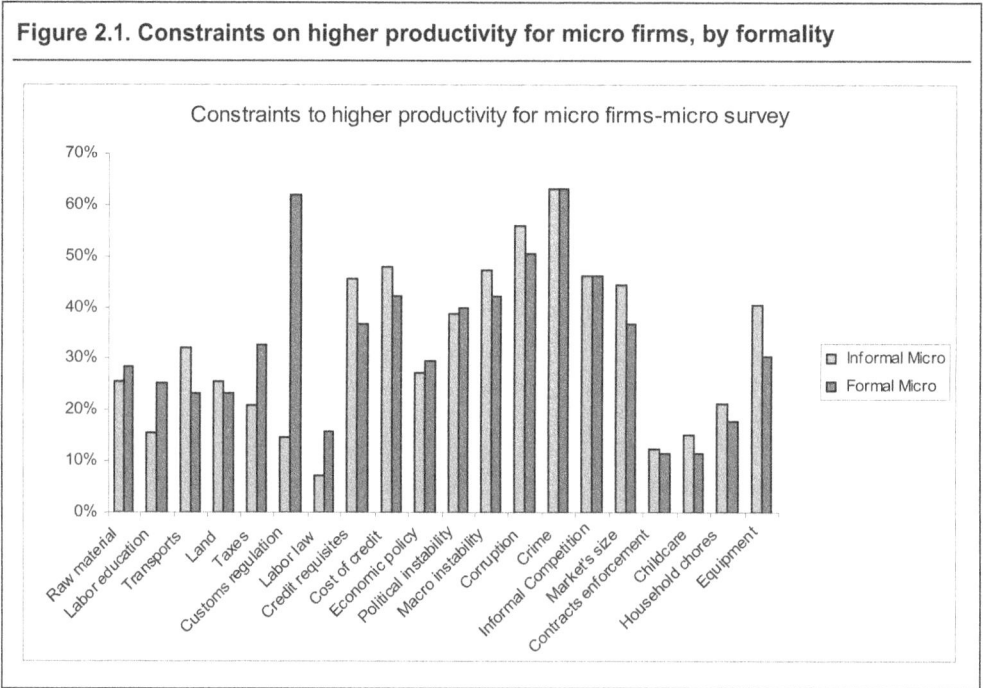

Source: World Bank micro-enterprise survey.

However, as firm size grows, there are more productive benefits to formality. Informal small firms report more constraints to productivity than formal small firms. Their top five constraints are related to corruption; exposure to crime, macro instability, cost of credit, and political instability. Formal small firms' top five constraints are macroeconomic instability, corruption, informal competition, crime, and political instability. Except for the cost of credit, which seems to affect more informal firms, both types of firms share similar constraints, though they rate them differently. Informal firms report, on average, more constraints to productivity. However, on specific issues related to taxes or informal competition, formal firms report more obstacles to productivity than informal firms (Figure 2.2).

As firms become even larger, the extent and type of constraints to productivity faced is even more pronounced, suggesting that effect of formality on productivity varies with the size of the firm. The small formal firms in the micro survey responded very similarly to small formal firms in the ICA, hence we use the ICA data on medium and large firms to investigate how productivity constraints evolve with size. It appears that medium and large firms face very similar constraints to functioning, which are quite different from the ones faced by small firms. Table 2.1 shows that the main constraint to the functioning of small formal firms is competition from the informal sector (32 percent), followed by political instability (27 percent) and access to finance (11 percent). For medium and large firms, the main obstacle is political instability (30 and 40 percent respectively), followed by competition from the informal sector (27 and 21 percent respectively), and then access to finance for medium firms (8 percent) and macroeconomic instability for large firms (12 percent).

Access to financial capital

Informal micro and small firms have access to a narrower set of formal financing mechanisms and at higher costs than formal firms. Informal firms are less likely to provide to a bank proper documentation, such as audited financial statements, government registration, and licensing. Informal firms may not register all assets as belonging to the company, so as to evade taxes or because they do not find it necessary to do so; hence their ability to use them as collateral for a loan may be limited.

Figure 2.2. Constraints on higher productivity for small firms, by formality

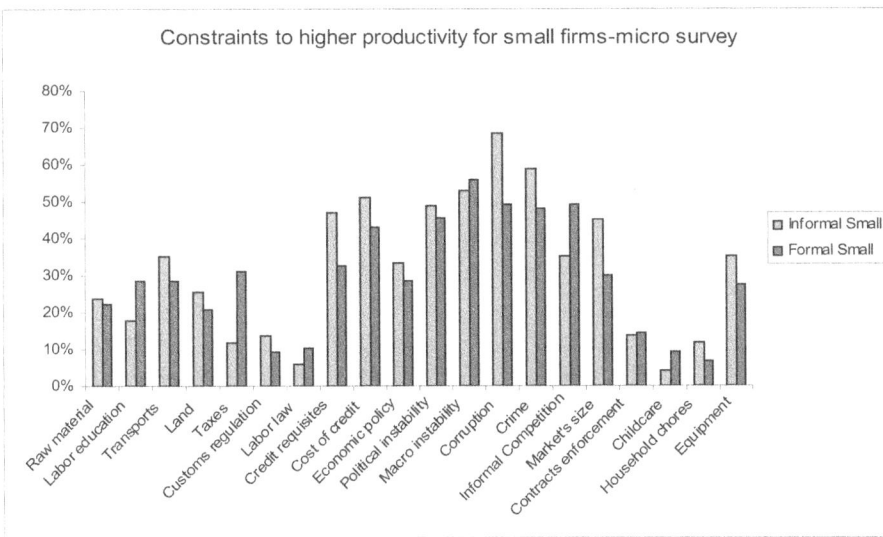

Source: World Bank micro-enterprise survey.

Table 2.1. Percentage of formal firms reporting the following factors as major constraints to their functioning, by size

	Small	Medium	Large
Competition from informal firms	32	27	21
Political instability	27	30	40
Access to finance	11	8	7
Macro instability	6	7	12
Corruption	5	7	4
Taxes	5	7	2
Crime and theft	3	2	2
Labor law	3	1	2
transport	2	4	2
Labor force	2	1	0
Obtaining licenses and permits	1	4	2
Customs regulation	1	1	2
Functioning of courts	0	1	1
Access to land	0	0	1

Source: Based on the ICA (2006) for Bolivia.
Note: The table presents the most serious constraint to the functioning of formal firms by size. The numbers are expressed in percentage of the sample.

Similarly, informal firms may try to evade taxes by hiding a fraction of their revenues or underreporting sales, so their financial statements may under represent the true profitability, financial soundness, and economic prospects of their firms. As a consequence informal firms may have less ability to get bank loans to finance working capital and new investment or equity capital from prospective investors (World Bank 2007, chapter 6).

Access to finance affects the productivity of micro and small firms, more than larger firms. The availability and cost of financing remains a serious constraint for their functioning, as compared with other constraints, especially when they are informal. See Figures 2.1 and 2.2 for the constraints to productivity for informal versus formal firms, which shows that for both micro and small informal firms access to credit (credit requisites and cost of credit) is more difficult than for formal firms.

Micro and small firms are more likely to fund their operating needs through microfinance institutions. The financial sector supplying credit to micro and small firms comprises two banks (Banco Solidario and Banco de Los Andes Procredit), private financial funds (PFF), savings and loan cooperatives (S&LC), as well as mutual savings and loan entities (MS&L). These entities offer a wide range of credit instruments, in terms of amount and purpose of loans, based on guarantees and estimated capacity for repayment. Though Bolivia's MFIs are among the least expensive in Latin America, the lack of proper documentation and underreporting of assets and profitability is still reflected in the prices prevailing in the microcredit market (21 percent nominal yearly interest rate for 2005, compared with 11 percent for traditional banking). However, this difference in interest rates is relatively small, considering that it is costlier and riskier to lend to a micro or small firm or an informal firm than to a larger firm. See Annex 2.1 comparing Bolivian to regional microfinance rates.

Improved asset registration, the formalization of operations, and a broader coverage of credit bureaus are keys to reducing credit costs and broadening access to credit. Improving the quality of financial statements (or reducing the costs of getting financial statements) would reduce the cost of credit and help increase the supply of credit. Such initiatives can also increase access to credit by broadening the demand of credit, by improving the quality of the applications for credit. Box 2.3 presents such initiatives in Bolivia.[3]

Box 2.3. Supply of credit to micro and small firms

The supply of credit is characterized by the wide range of financial instruments offered by microfinance institutions, commercial banks, private financial funds, and cooperatives operating in services and production sectors. The amount available to a micro enterprise varies from US$100 up to US$30,000, or a certain percentage of clients' net equity (up to 3 percent in some cases). Lending to small enterprises implies substantially larger amounts, up to US$50,000, and the borrowers are usually required to present financial statements and property insurance. In contrast, micro firms need to submit only operating time requirements (at least one year, in some cases six months) or residential water or energy bills.

The term of the loans varies according to the purpose of the credit. Short-term credit is most common, with terms between one and seven months, but in some cases up to two years for operating capital or three years for investment capital. BancoSol and FIE S.A. extend terms up to five years for capital investments. Contrary to traditional banking credit, micro credit amortizations are very flexible, taking into account the nature of the client's operations and its repayment capacity. The scope of guarantees is wide as well. For instance, the most frequent are personal guarantees, pledged collateral with or without dispossession, certificate of deposits, or mortgages. Sometimes the loan can be classified as an unsecured debt. In the case of new clients without credit history, most of the microfinance institutions offer group guarantees and other type of credit from U$100 up to US$3,000 by member. Some institutions may require additional criteria regarding the dispersion between the lower and higher amount lent within a group. Former clients may benefit from special financial instruments. Pro Mujer allows its best female entrepreneur clients (based on credit history) to borrow individually up to US$15,000 at terms between 6 and 48 months. At FIE, former clients with good credit history are allowed to use lines of revolving credit for 36 months in order to finance investments in capital and operating capital.

During the past year, the Bank and Insurance Superintendency (SBEF) has strengthened the regulatory framework for MFIs, PFFs, and SLCs to help them better respond to the dynamics of market's characteristics. The SBEF has also promoted the creation of Credit Information Bureaus (BIC) (ENSERBIC in Santa Cruz and INFOCRED in La Paz), which establish a credit information network across regulated entities or across unregulated ones. BICs have increased microcredit transparency and decreased the information asymmetry and hence the costs of providing credit to micro and small firms.

Low access to credit from financial institutions forces informal firms (even more so than formal firms) to rely on their own savings, followed by loans from family and friends and then by sector supplier credit. From the focus groups, it appears that supplier credit can include grocery stores or *tiendas de barrios* getting inputs from Coca

Cola or the beer company Quilmes Incesa (particularly around holidays), and advances from clients (for the manufacturing of wooden furniture and handicrafts). Interviewed firms and those surveyed in the 2006 ICA found the financial system too slow to react and not enabling firms to seize business opportunities. They also felt that the banking system lacked flexibility in dealing with micro and small firms in terms of the repayment schedules, the amount and maturity of loans, and the procedures to get a loan.

Firms interviewed complained about the high cost of credit, comparing getting a credit to lifetime bondage. Comments included "Taking out a loan is to get in debt for life" and "If I take out a loan, I work only to pay the bank and not to live." Interviewees noted a tradeoff between dealing with the bureaucracy and procedures of a commercial bank, and getting a better interest rate, versus paying much higher interest rates to MFIs, but with simpler procedures. Hence, the higher costs of MFIs are offset somewhat by their greater understanding of micro and small firms, less cumbersome requirements, and more flexible repayment procedures. However, the average interest rate of micro loans in Bolivia is the lowest of the region, and so firms' complaints about the high cost of capital may reflect a lack of productive projects and unrealistic expectations about what the cost of borrowing should be.

Access to credit largely depends on the size of the firm, its client base, its access to export markets, and collateral guarantees. In all sectors, bigger firms (such as the upper quartile of small firms) could get a credit line from a bank; a medium-size small firm could get credit from an MFI. In contrast, the lower quartiles of small firms and most micro firms would rely on their own savings, reinvested profits, loans from friends and family, advances from clients, or mechanisms of collective savings as the main source of financing of working capital and new investment. This is particularly true for wood furniture, camelid clothing, and transport firms. Firms that had a bigger demand for their products, as a result of either higher turnover from the domestic demand (like in *tiendas de barrios* with good location) or greater access to exporting markets, had a better access to credit from MFIs, banks, and their suppliers. For firms within the same industry, access also depends on whether the firm exports or belongs to an association or union (like in transport). Food sales enterprises employing less than five persons report the least access to credit from financial institutions. However, they use a type of rotating saving system called *pasanaku* to save.[4]

Guarantees determine the amount of credit obtained, but also the terms of credit. For instance, if the guarantee is important relative to the size of the loan, the bank will allow a credit line and a longer maturity to repay the loan. If the guarantee is less sizable, the amount of the loan is reduced and the maturity shortened. As a consequence, once a firm has a guarantee, it will use the credit for the investment purposes that suit the firm best, regardless of what was stated as the initial purpose of the loan. Guarantees are both personal and physical. In the transport sector, firms use the membership in a union or an association as guarantee to get joint bank credit. Membership also serves as a fiduciary guarantee and as a guarantee to be a monopoly service provider in certain routes.

To complement micro finance lending, the development of new financial instruments should provide deeper access to credit in the long term. In the medium term, the development of financial instruments, such as leases, warrants, factoring, and reciprocal guarantees, could help widen access to finance for firms. Most micro and small firms interviewed said that they were waiting for the government-proposed low interest rates loans to finance micro, small firms, and small producers.

Access to physical capital

The acquisition and maintenance of equipment and physical capital is strongly impeded by low access to financing mechanisms. Firms from the focus group report the lack of financing to purchase the equipment as an important constraint on their functioning and productivity. And when they are able to buy the equipment, the productive value of the equipment ultimately depends on their ability to get replacement parts.

There is a tradeoff between price and quality for replacement parts. Parts from China tend to be more affordable but do not last long, whereas secondhand parts from the original maker are more expensive but last longer. In particular, in transport of passengers and products, secondhand cars imported from Japan via Chile and Brazil and *chatarras* (cars destined for junkyards) have proved a good source for parts, at the expense of road safety and air quality.

There is evidence that informal firms are more likely to use informal suppliers, especially under VAT regimes. Informality is propagated along the supply chains, and entire informal supply chains are created. Those chains are harder to formalize and constitute severe barriers to competition and to entry for any formal firms in the chain (Scheinkman and de Paula 2006).

Atomization and specialization prevent firms from pooling to buy equipment. Interviews in the wood sector illustrate the atomization of informal micro and small firms and the lack of financial instruments to finance new investment. Small firms are unable to get together to buy ovens to dry the wood, because ovens are calibrated on the type of wood exploited, and the firms all exploit different types of wood. Hence, big producers control both the quality and price of wood, segmenting themselves from small producers in the quality of the output. In small restaurants, firms cannot pool to buy freezers and other equipment reportedly because "the needs of equipment for a fish restaurant are different from a meat restaurant." Trust or lack thereof is also cited as a reason for not associating to buy equipment. However, a better legal environment to enforce judicial contracts and expedite recovery of assets through litigation should help alleviate trust issues.

Given the scale of production and the size of demand, leasing could be a useful instrument to increase access to credit. Some interviewed firms complain that the lack of industrial machines prevents them from responding to an increase in demand when opportunity knocks at the door. However, the average day-to-day demand is quite small, justifying an equally small production response, since small firms do not want to carry significant inventories. It is hard to justify the investment in industrial machines to step up production when demand is not steady. In such an environment, leasing could be useful, in combination with group guarantees to increase available equipment for micro and small firms to scale up production in times of increased demand. A new leasing law is currently under consideration by Congress; its passage would mark a major step in alleviating access to physical capital for firms.

Access to land is affected by scarce financing mechanisms. Very few firms are able to buy the locale where they operate. In retail grocery stores and food sales, location is essential, and firms have expressed their hope to be able to own their locale, but only a handful of the bigger and more successful actually do. Most others start in the street, then rent a small locale, and then try to buy it or expand to other locations. The difficult access to finance for working capital and new investment further impedes the process of acquiring their first locale and then using it as collateral for future credits.

Access to labor and human capital

The labor productivity of informal firms is often very low. Productivity at the firm level can be defined as the output (physical or value added adjusted for service/quality differences) over labor input (hours worked, units of physical capital). Informal firms are relatively labor intensive because the relative cost of labor they face is lower than for formal firms. Hence, labor productivity represents most of the productivity of informal firms. According to McKinsey Global Institute (2002), labor inputs in developing countries represent more than 65 percent of total inputs, with capital accounting for the remainder. In some sectors, such as utilities (telecommunications, power) capital accounts for more than 80 percent of total input.

Higher labor productivity is associated with less informality. There is regional evidence that firms with higher levels of labor productivity exhibit lower rates of tax and social security evasion, for a given firm size and time in business (World Bank 2007). The effects are significant for workers underreporting in Bolivia. For all other countries in the region, doubling of the firm's labor productivity is associated with underreporting rates that are on average 2 percentage points lower (World Bank 2007). Finally, medium firms are more affected by the inadequately educated workforce (31 percent report it as an important or major constraint), compared with 24 percent for small or large firms.[5]

Labor productivity of workers depends on firm size and access to finance. Evidence from the focus group suggests that the bigger the firm, the more it can afford to function in a more professional manner, including hiring of qualified workers and outsourcing of a qualified accountant for bookkeeping. MFIs also provide training to their customers in accounting, business management, and marketing, which helps them modernize business operations and become more productive. Smaller and micro firms are less likely to attract qualified workers, because they cannot offer them good career prospects or competitive salaries. To compensate for these shortcomings, smaller firms have adopted a system of on-the-job training for their workers. However, once the apprentices have acquired skills, they tend to move to better jobs. The issue of labor retention particularly affects food stands and mini restaurants.

Exporting firms have higher labor productivity. Firms with access to export markets, such as wooden furniture and camelid clothing makers, report more skilled workers and seem to manage their business in a more professional way, often outsourcing accountants for their bookkeeping. Those firms are also bigger than the average firm in their sector and often have access to finance. This suggests that labor productivity seems to increase with the demand that the firm faces, more productive firms attracting more productive workers. Small food vendors, in contrast, have no access to complimentary training, and they cannot afford to pay for the training. In addition, firms that do not have access to MFIs cannot benefit from the training offered to clients.

The informal sector acts as an escape valve for a low-productivity formal sector in some sectors, according to the focus group results. The transport and grocery stores sectors seem to constitute an escape valve for the overall economy, attracting all those who could not find a job in the formal sector. Interviewees made comments such as "All the unemployed think about driving a taxi or selling goods." This is due to the low barriers of entry in those sectors. For instance, in transport, the low cost of *chutos* (imported secondhand cars) allows an easier entry to the informal transport sector. However, the transfer of knowledge from the previous job to the new one is not guaranteed, as the previous job often has little to do with cars, transport, or mechanics. In contrast, in grocery stores, educated newcomers are more likely to use their previous education or training to improve their productivity in the new job. As a consequence, workers in the transport sector often see the job as a temporary step toward a better and more stable one, whereas workers in *tiendas de barrios* see their new job as more permanent. Hence, in transport, workers do not have many incentives to invest in improving productivity, and firm owners do not have incentives to train them.

Labor productivity depends less on formal education than on the years of experience working in the sector and the reason for getting into the business. In many sectors, interviewed people reported entering the productive force when they were young by working with relatives in a family business or in another segment of the same productive chain. This is often the case with camelid clothing and wood furniture manufacturers, *tiendas de barrio,* and small eateries. By contrast, entry to the textile manufacturing sector is usually not through the family, but is an individual and opportunistic decision. This sector is also particular in that workers have a minimum of five years experience or more on average. In addition, most received training from the financial sector and also from textile firms in Argentina through temporary migration. The acquired knowledge makes it harder for a newcomer without prior experience in the sector to enter and be successful. As a consequence, this sector ranks access to capital, rather than labor productivity, on top of their list of constraints to increase their productivity.

Access to raw material and the supply chain

Productivity, clientele, and exporting possibilities hinge on the quality of inputs found in the local market. The focus groups suggest that access to good-quality inputs is an issue for all firms, but is more acute for informal firms because of their atomization, which means they cannot pool and directly negotiate with providers. Informal firms are price and quantity takers of whatever they are supplied. In a sector like wooden furniture, the main input (wood) is locally produced. However, there is segmentation between the domestic market and the exporting market. The domestic market gets the leftovers of the export market; it is supplied with noncertified and nonstandardized wood. This segmentation of inputs affects the quality of the end product and hence its retail value and potential for export. In sectors such as textiles and camelids, the domestic production of thread has not reached the quality standards and variety expected from the market, as well as a competitive price level. Hence firms turn to imported inputs. The quality of the inputs depends on the country of origin (Korean fabrics and Chilean wool are sought after), and the expertise of the importing intermediary in selecting good products and bringing them safely in the local market.

The monopolistic behavior of retailers and intermediaries increases the costs of inputs. As a result of their small scale and atomization, micro and small firms provision themselves from intermediaries. In some cases, informal firms have tried to pool and cut out the middle man, but they were not able to negotiate better prices than they could get from intermediaries. In other cases, the fact that the input was produced abroad rendered negotiations with the foreign producer difficult. It appears that in all the six sectors considered, intermediaries are controlled by monopolies or oligopolies, meaning that the variety of supply is limited and the quality of supply depends of the goodwill of the monopoly. For instance, in grocery stores (*tiendas de barrios*), Coca Cola has the biggest presence in soft drinks' distribution. Pepsi has a much smaller market share. However, Coca Cola's distribution services are reportedly most professional and efficient, with the company even offering opportunities for training to some firms, but the firms must also agree not to offer other products. In contrast, some other monopolies have less than satisfactory services, as is the case in the distribution of milk.

Quality, technology, and competition

The lack of product quality control in most informal firms can jeopardize the sector. Informal firms are not visited by municipal inspections; hence the quality of goods produced in the informal sector varies depending on the producer. From the focus group survey, it appears that in the wood sector, access to quality-controlled wood is limited for the local market, affecting the quality of input and hence productivity, as well as the price of the end product. Interviews in grocery stores suggest that in the past clients have rejected altered products, such as alcoholic beverages and cigarettes, because of municipalities' awareness campaigns. Hence, firms interviewed are more careful about checking the original seals of the products and provisioning themselves from legal sources

There seems to be a void in the adoption of new technology to improve productivity, which may indicate scope for public intervention. Limited access to training and equipment is an important constraint for technology diffusion. Micro and small firms use artisan methods and rustic machines rather than industrial ones, as mentioned in the physical capital section above. In Asia, public interventions to increase small businesses' dynamism were most efficient in the development of technology centers and the diffusion and adoption of new technologies (Iqbal and Urata 2002).

Demand is mostly local, as many micro and small firms usually cannot meet most quality and professional standards to export. In the case of camelid clothing makers, the demand from the exporting markets has increased, whereas local demand has shrunk. Hence, the domestic supply responds to the irregular demands of the local clients. Firms in many sectors (wood, textiles, camelid clothing) complain about the lack of standardization that prevents them from producing in series and reaching capacity and quality norms to access more important markets. The lack of industrial equipment is also an impediment to reach higher production levels. Policies to induce business owners to replicate products for different specification, as is done in Peru, could increase the productivity of the firms.

Competition from formal and informal firms is extremely strong. There are no formal barriers to entry or formal regulations for many sectors, meaning almost anybody can set up shop and compete. In addition, the lack of property rights allows the competition to copy products at no risk. Hence, competition is on price, quality, innovation, location, and services. As a consequence, profits are driven to a minimum, and those who cannot compete quickly go out of business. This, coupled with the monopoly position of input providers, makes it a tough game for any firm to be successful. In some cases, competition from other informal firms is accompanied by competition from formal medium or even large firms. For instance, *tiendas de barrios* compete with each other (on location), with mini markets (on variety), and with supermarkets (on price and quality).

All firms, regardless of size, are affected by "informal competition," but small firms seem to feel it the most. Based on the ICA data, small firms report that competition from the informal sector is the most important obstacle to their functioning (32 percent of the sample). By comparison, medium and large firms report that it is the second-most important obstacle to their functioning (27 percent of medium firms and 21 percent of large firms). Some of the reported competition from the informal sector, however, may just be competition in general.

In some sectors, competition extends to exporting firms. In wood and camelid clothing manufacturing, the main competitors are other domestic exporting firms and foreign firms exporting similar products. In wood, larger exporting firms get the best cut wood input. Smaller local producers with access to second-rate wood cannot compete and are shut out of the export market. In camelid clothing, Peruvian firms are the main competitors in the export market. Reportedly, the quality of the Peruvian fiber has tremendously improved, thanks to an aggressive national policy to develop and industrialize the sector and to improve the quality and variety of the fiber. Furthermore, Peru markets its products internationally through renowned designers and by participating in international forums. As a result, they have been able to achieve better access to most exporting markets. The local clothing sector has been inundated by used clothing from the United States, which has almost eradicated domestic demand for locally made clothing. A policy to regulate the entry of used clothing will greatly help the firms in those sectors regain a share of domestic demand. The government is leading a productive conversion policy for used clothes sellers, promising them financing through the development bank, and training if they convert to another economic activity. So far, 350 firms have converted.

Gender and productivity

The productivity of female entrepreneurs is lower than the productivity of their male counterpart due to many factors. Female entrepreneurs operate at a lower scale and earn less than their male counterpart. The lower scale of operation is due to the fact that they dedicate less labor (hours worked) and capital to their business. In some cases, the lower scale is voluntary so as to enable them to take care of other household duties. In other cases, the business is complementary to other activities of the household like agricultural activities. The level of education is also lower for female entrepreneurs than for male entrepreneurs.

Removing constraints to capital for female entrepreneurs can be very profitable depending on the sector of activity. Estimating the internal rate of return of doubling the capital of the firm in each of the six sectors, by gender shows that: in food sales, clothes manufacturing, and camelid products, returns are expected to be higher for women than for men. In contrast, further investment in the transport sector and in grocery stores does not appear to be attractive for female entrepreneurs (see Table 2.2). Box 2.4 presents in more details why women may choose to operate at lower scale to balance their need for flexibility and their lower aptitude for risk. The box also highlights the difference among sectors of their desire to grow.

Table 2.2. Internal rates of return for a doubling of capital, by sector and gender

	Clothes manufacturing	Transportation	Grocery stores	Food sales	Wood products	Camelid products
Men	9%	−10%	4%	32%	2%	4%
Women	27%	−13%	−7%	37%	4%	18%

Source: Author's estimation based on information in the 2007 micro and small enterprise survey.

Box 2.4. Constraints to higher productivity for female entrepreneurs

---

Female entrepreneurs operate on a smaller scale. One explanation is that they do not have the capital to expand, but another possible explanation is that they do not want to grow, because the business then would loose some of the features that make a micro-business particularly attractive for women (not to depend on others, to be able to care for children simultaneously, flexible working hours). When asked about what they consider the ideal number of employees for their business five years into the future, the average for women is 6.9 compared to 9.2 for men. For grocery stores in particular, women have already reached what they consider the ideal size (2.8 employees, on average) and do not want additional employees. This is in contrast to men, who would like bigger stores with about 10 employees. Also, according to the micro enterprise survey results, women have less confidence than men in their ability to hire and manage employees that are not family members. An exception is the case of women in textiles who have a stronger desire to expand. While male entrepreneurs in this sector would like to double the number of employees from 5 to 10, female entrepreneurs would like to expand from an average of 2 to 13 employees. In this sector, each additional employee requires a capital investment of approximately Bs. 8.800. Thus, the average female entrepreneur would need to make an additional investment of close to Bs. 100,000 (14 times their present capital) in order to reach their desired number of employees. From a simple regression, we find that a 100 percent increase in capital would tend to increase monthly profits by about 22 percent. Given that women in this sector currently have average monthly profits of about Bs. 755 and average capital of Bs. 7.267, an additional investment of Bs. 7.267 would yield a monthly benefit of about Bs. 166. This implies an internal rate of return on the investment of about 27 percent, which means that it would likely be worth borrowing money for.

(Box continues on next page)

Box 2.4 (continued)

Female entrepreneurs operate in low-profitability sectors. The food sales sector is dominated by women, as they have a much larger experience with food preparation. Moreover, the sector requires relatively little investment and education, but yields relatively high profits. Grocery stores are attractive to women despite the long working hours and low salary because it allows them not to depend on others (neither bosses nor employees), they can simultaneously care for children, and the business can grow slowly with minimum risk. The camelid product sector pays lower monthly profits than the other sectors, but women also dedicate much less time and capital to it, and have much lower levels of education, so this activity is likely considered complementary to domestic and agricultural activities. The clothes manufacturing sector is almost equally divided between male and female entrepreneurs, but women earn much less than men. Again this is due to the much smaller scale of operations. Women, on average, work 19 hours less than men each week, have invested less than half the capital, and have less than half the number of employees, so it is not strange that their monthly profits are also less than half those of men in the sector. The hourly wage is relatively high, though: at Bs. 7.5/hour it is higher than for women in any other sector than food sales.

Female entrepreneurs are more likely to hire women. In every single sector analyzed, female entrepreneurs tend to hire more women than their male counterparts. On average, for male entrepreneurs only 15 percent of employees are women, while for female entrepreneurs 82 percent are women. This means that female entrepreneurs can be an important source of employment for other women. However, these female employees may be less educated, with lower marginal productivity and lower salaries.

Source: World Bank micro-enterprises survey (2007).

In sum, access to capital seems to be the main and overarching constraint to higher productivity for all micro and small firms, and even more so for informal ones. Access to finance provides better inputs, working capital, and new investment funding, and it supports maintenance of equipment and training for employers. However, despite the competitive rates in the microfinance industry, many micro firms do not get access to those loans, or still find their costs too burdening. Next in importance, access to inputs seems to be a constraint affecting micro and small firms, as they do not have access to good-quality inputs from the local markets and they suffer from monopolistic intermediaries. Third, access to skilled workers affects the productivity of micro and small firms, hence public provision of business management and sector-specific productivity modules should help to alleviate this constraint. Finally, public policies can promote and support internal and external demand, through expanded public investment to support the marketing of Bolivian products abroad. The public sector also has a role to play in the diffusion and adoption of technology to support micro and small firms' development in those sectors. There is scope for public-private and private-private partnership programs between micro and small firms and larger firms. For instance, in Asia there is evidence that clustering and subcontracting promote small firms' dynamism and development, but the evidence hinges on the sector of operation.[6]

How Is the Operational, Regulatory, and Institutional Environment Constraining Productivity?

The operational, regulatory, and institutional environment seems to be more hostile to informal firms, because of their small size, than to formal firms. Operational constraints are related to the costs of registering and operating a business. Because informal firms are on average smaller, the costs of procedures to register a firm are relatively more important for them, and very small firms may not be able to navigate complex procedures. Petty corruption and red tape is a particularly important operational constraint affecting informal firms. They are at the mercy of legal or illegal fines, harassment, and lack of compliance with private agreements by their suppliers, clients, or workers.[7] The institutional and regulatory framework originally aimed at protecting workers through labor laws, social protection, business customs, and trade regulation has proved unfavorable to most firms. It particularly affects informal micro and small firms, as they are de facto excluded from protection of labor and business laws and courts of justice.

The operational, regulatory, and institutional environment affects firms' functioning and productivity differently, depending on their size. Small, medium, and large firms perceive different obstacles to their functioning from their business environment, although some constraints affect all firms regardless of size (Table 2.3).

Table 2.3. Constraints on firms' productivity posed by the operational, regulatory, and institutional environment, by firm size

Constraints that affect firms the same way regardless of size		Constraints that affect firms differently depending on their size	
More binding for small firms	*More binding for large firms*	*More binding for small firms*	*More binding for large firms*
Telecom/Electricity	Telecom/Electricity		Tax rates ***
Trade/Customs regulations			Tax administration*
Labor regulation, regulation on pricing and mark ups	Labor regulation, regulation on pricing and mark ups		Regulation on the hours of operations*
Competition of the informal sector	Competition of the informal sector	Business licensing and permits*	
Access to land	Access to land	Access to finance ***	
Corruption	Functioning of the courts	Inadequately educated workforce*	
Crime, theft, and disorder	Crime, theft, and disorder		
Macroeconomic and political instability	Macroeconomic and political instability		

Source: ICA Data 2006.

Note: The table presents constraints that affect firms the same way regardless of their size and constraints that affect firms differently, depending on their size. The tests conducted are chi square statistical significance test between size (small, medium, and large) and the grade of obstacle the constraint presents for the functioning of the firm (none, minor, moderate, important, major). Statistical significance is represented by * at 1%, ** at 5%, and *** at 10% respectively.

The tests conducted are chi square tests to determine whether there is a significant statistical relation between size (small, medium, and large) and the grade of obstacle the constraint presents for the functioning of the firm (none, minor, moderate, important, major).

Operational constraints

Macroeconomic and political instability were the major constraint to firm functioning in Bolivia in 2005, according to the ICA data (2006). In Bolivia, 2005 was characterized by prolonged political and economic instability, with blockades and strikes. Hence, it is not surprising that the ICA, conducted in 2005–06, reports for all firms, regardless of their size, that political and economic instability was the most important constraint to their functioning.

Business registration and licensing are perceived as more of an obstacle to small and medium firms than large firms. A somewhat greater share of small and medium firms than large firms report registration and licensing as an important to major obstacle (14 percent versus 10 percent, according to data from the ICA 2006). The focus group interviews further confirm the lack of knowledge of registration locations and procedures for almost all informal micro and small firms interviewed (except those exporting in camelids and the manufacturing of wood furniture). The International Finance Corporation (IFC) has targeted the reduction and simplification of municipal procedures to register firms as a means of reducing informality. This effort is particularly important given that a firm starting without a formal registration is associated with rates of tax and social security evasion that are between 6 and 25 percent higher than for firms that registered at the time of start up (World Bank 2007).

When a firm starts informal, chances are higher that it will remain informal in some dimensions, perpetuating a cycle of informality, which may be broken only by increasing formalization at the onset. Thus, policies to simplify registration and licensing of business have the potential to reduce informality not only immediately but also in the future, as fewer firms will be starting as informal. A first step would be to focus on simplifying and reducing the costs of renewing licenses annually, which firms report as the more bothersome procedure related to being formal (Figure 2.3).

Most firms, regardless of size, agree that infrastructure and access to telecommunications, electricity, and land are minor obstacles to functioning. Firms interviewed in the focus group did not complain about those issues. The main reason might be that both the ICA and the focus groups were conducted in major urban areas (El Alto, La Paz, Cochabamba, and Santa Cruz). Hence, they might not be representative of the constraints faced by firms in rural areas, for which these issues might be more important.

Crime and disorder represent major obstacle to functioning for micro and small firms. Crime and theft are lower in Bolivia than in many other countries of Latin America. The firms survey conducted for the study reveals that crime and disorder ranks top on the lists of constraints to productivity for micro firms regardless of their formality status. See Figures 2.1 and 2.2. The focus group interviews found that the provision of inputs for restaurant and food sales businesses in El Alto was sometimes disrupted by blockages and strikes. This type of disruption is also captured by the political instability variable (see Table 2.2). Informal firms interviewed in the transport

Figure 2.3. Constraints on registration and licensing at the municipal level

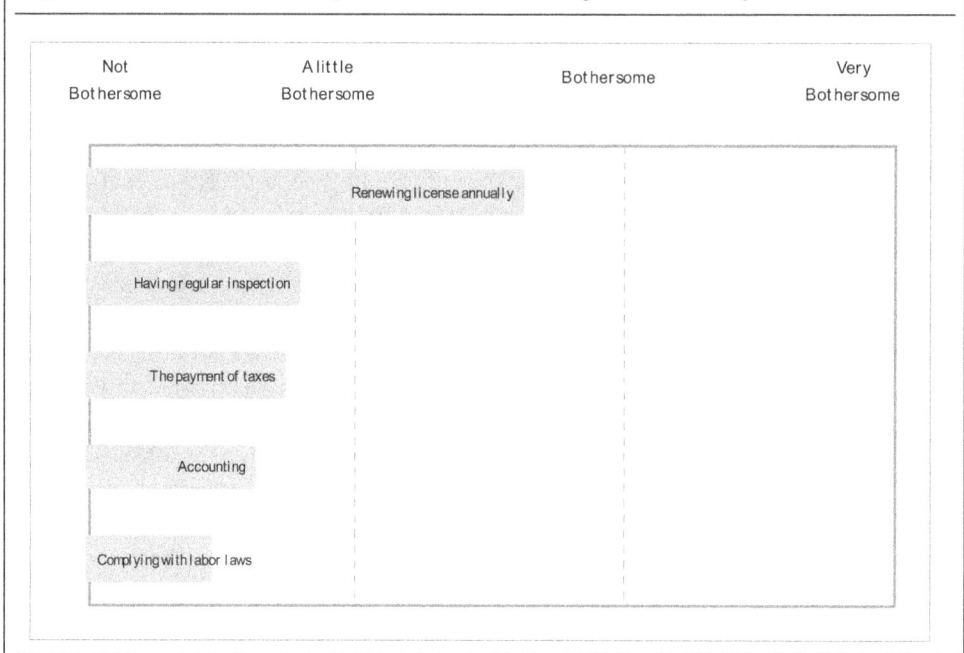

Not Bothersome	A little Bothersome	Bothersome	Very Bothersome

Renewing license annually

Having regular inspection

The payment of taxes

Accounting

Complying with labor laws

Source: IFC Municipal Scorecards report for Bolivia 2007.

sector focus group reported that the affiliation with a union was also an insurance against crime, especially in cities such as Santa Cruz.

Institutional and regulatory constraints

The majority of all firms, regardless of size, consider corruption a major obstacle. Two thirds of small firms consider corruption as an important or major obstacle to their functioning, compared with 62 percent of medium firms and 55 percent of large firms (ICA 2006). However, when compared with other obstacles, such as access to finance, competition of the informal sector, or political instability, corruption is not as salient for all firms.

By contrast, the functioning of the courts does not represent an obstacle to the functioning of firms. Though the differences are not statistically significant, large firms seem more concerned with the functioning of the courts than small or medium firms. Indeed, 16 percent of large firm perceived that the functioning of courts represent an important obstacle to their functioning compared with 8 percent of small firms and 9 percent of medium firms. This may be due to the fact that large firms are more likely to go to court, not only because they enter into formal contracts more often than smaller firms, but also because they are more likely to know how to fight "abusive" fines than small or micro firms (World Bank 2001).

The tax burden affects more large firms than micro and small firms. The tax rates and the tax administration affect more large firms (34 percent report it as an important to major constraint) than small firms (with only 26 percent reporting it as an important to major constraint) (ICA 2006). As for tax payments, the average time to comply with tax requirements for a limited liability firm (large firm) is more than 1,000 hours of labor, compared with a regional average of 430 hours. The total tax rate represents 80 percent of profits, much higher than the regional average of 50 percent (World Bank 2005c). The simplified regime for small firms, though fast, cheap, and not requiring accounting books, does not allow the discount on VAT receipts for input purchases; hence it fails to be attractive to small firms. Many of the recommendations to increase formalization in Bolivia suggest a reform of the tax environment for a simpler and friendlier tax regime for micro and small firms (DFID DECMA 2007; ICA 2001).

Costly partnership incorporation remains an obstacle for small firms to reach economies of scales by association. The certificate of incorporation (*certificado de personería jurídica*) is not easy to obtain in Bolivia because of the multitude of requirements and the length of the process (8–10 months). This hurdle often discourages individual entrepreneurs willing to pool with others to scale up production or undertake bigger project (World Bank 2001).

The labor environment in Bolivia is often qualified as restrictive. The Doing Business 2006 ranking of Bolivia illustrates those rigidities. The difficulty of firing index is at 100, the highest possible ranking, compared with 26.5 for Latin America as a whole; firing costs are also very high at almost 100 weeks of salary, compared with 60 for the region. However, evidence from the ICA 2006 suggests that labor regulations are overall not a major constraint to the functioning of firms, and all firms regardless of size share that opinion.

As a consequence of costly trade and customs regulations, few firms have access to important export markets, which is particularly important given the limited size of the domestic market. The costs and time to import and export in Bolivia are higher than the regional average, as are the numbers of documents required.[8] However, according to the ICA 2006 data for Bolivia, most firms, regardless of size, perceive that it is not a constraint to their functioning. Most informal firms are not targeting the export market, and the minority who are did not report trade and customs regulation as a constraint to their activity, as they are indirect exporters.

In sum, some operational, regulatory, and institutional constraints seem to affect micro and small firms in Bolivia more than larger firms. The most important constraints are related to the business licensing and permits registration, the tax administration and tax rates, the inadequately educated workforce. Other constraints initially thought as important were perceived by micro and small firms not as a constraint to their functioning or productivity. Those constraints are related to the labor, trade, and customs regulation; crime, theft, and disorder; and access to land, telecommunications, and electricity. Of those constraints that affect all firms, some such as corruption and the competition of the informal sector constitute a major obstacle to the functioning of micro and small firms.

Conclusions

Regional evidence shows a negative correlation between productivity and informality, which suggests that the more productive a firm, the less likely it is to keep operating irregularly. However, productivity is affected by many variables in addition to whether firms operate formally or informally—access to inputs, the production function, and technology strongly influences productivity, as does the operational, regulatory, and institutional environment. Focus group interviews of informal micro and small firms in six sectors show these conclusions:

- Access to capital seems to be the main and overarching constraint to higher productivity for micro and small firms, and the access and cost of finance are in turn related to informality.
- Access to inputs constrains the productivity of micro and small firms, as they do not have access to good-quality inputs from the local markets, and they suffer from the monopolistic dictatorship of intermediaries. As a result, informal firms may need to buy informal inputs in some cases, propagating informality along the productive chain.
- Access to skilled workers is also a constraint, especially for micro firms. Public provision of business management and sector-specific productivity modules should help to alleviate this constraint.
- Public policy has a role to play in the diffusion and adoption of technology, by supporting the development of micro and small firms, as well as the creation of public-private and private-private partnership programs. Public policies should also promote and support internal and external demand, through expanded public investment to support the marketing of Bolivian products abroad. The case of Peru in the development of the camelid fiber and the marketing of camelid products can be a useful example for Bolivia
- Some operational, regulatory, and institutional constraints seem to affect micro and small firms more than other firms. These obstacles in the business environment are related to the complexity of business licensing and permits registration, the lax enforcement of tax administration and tax rates, and the inadequately educated workforce.
- Corruption and the competition of the informal sector are also major constraints in the functioning and productivity of micro and small firms. Hence, policies to increase the productivity and the formalization of micro and small firms should take into account the distorting effect that they might have on the competition with formal firms.

Notes

[1] It is an annual fee to be paid by each establishment performing any kind of commercial activity to the municipality. This fee in addition to the license fee paid when registering in the municipality (*Padron municipal de Contribuyentes*). The license of operation must be renewed every three years.

[2] Daily tax paid by street sellers who use public property to the municipality.

[3] The supply of credit section is based on input from Jean Clevy (Central Bank of Nicaragua and World Bank).

[4] In the *pasanaku* system, every day members give the collecting agent 10 Bolivianos (US$1.20), and pay him 60 centavos, and every 50 days they are repaid Bs. 500. Hence members pay Bs. 30 per 50 days to have someone else save for them.

[5] See data Bolivia ICA (2006).

[6] See Iqbal and Urata 2002. Clustering, which refers to the geographic concentration of interconnecting companies in particular business fields, has proved particularly successful in increasing the productivity of small firms in Indonesia and Japan by providing specialization, ease of procurement, diffusion of technology, and public policy support. In this case, policy support provided by regional local government in the form of public testing, research, and technology development centers seems to make a difference.

[7] Formal and larger firms are more likely to contest fines, and the high rate at which these fines are overturned in the favor of firms suggests that fines are often unfounded. However, informal firms will not dare to take action. See World Bank (2001).

[8] See Doing Business 2007: the cost to export (import) is US$1,110 per container (US$1,230) compared to US$1,068 for the regional average (US$1,226). The number of documents required in order to export or import is 12 compared to 7.3 to export and 9.5 to import at the regional level.

Annex 2.1. Interest rates for microcredit institutions in Bolivia and other Latin American countries (at end June 2005)

FINCOMUN	Mexico	114,26%
COMPARTAMOS	Mexico	100,18%
FDD	Rep.Dominicana	83,65%
ADOPEM	Rep.Dominicana	67,07%
IDESI LA LIBERTAD	Peru	63,05%
FRAC	Mexico	61,24%
PROMUJER	Nicaragua	58,34%
ADRA PERU	Peru	57,86%
PROMUJER PERU	Peru	56,67%
D-MIRO	Ecuador	46,08%
CREAR AREQUIPA	Peru	45,34%
PROCREDIT	Nicaragua	43,68%
MIDE	Peru	43,22%
EL COMERCIO	Paraguay	43,00%
CONFIANZA	Peru	42,36%
WWB POPAYAN	Colombia	41,84%
CMAC SULLANA	Peru	41,73%
WWB BOGOTA	Colombia	41,68%
EDYFICAR	Peru	41,15%
PROMUJER BOLIVIA	Bolivia	39,83%
PROEMPRESA	Peru	39,74%
NIEBOROWSKI	Nicaragua	39,25%
NUEVA VISION	Peru	39,11%
CREAR TACNA	Peru	39,00%
CMAC ICA	Peru	38,84%
WWB CALI	Colombia	37,55%
WWB BUCARAMANGA	Colombia	35,60%
AMC	El Salvador	35,54%
FUNDESER	Nicaragua	34,89%
CMAC AREQUIPA	Peru	32,63%
CMAC TRUJILLO	Peru	31,50%
WWB MEDELLIN	Colombia	31,41%
CMAC TACNA	Peru	30,06%
D-FRIF	Bolivia	29,71%
CMAC CUSCO	Peru	28,15%
BANCO PROCREDIT	El Salvador	21,53%
ASOFIN (1)	Bolivia	21,23%
FADES	Bolivia	20,71%

CHAPTER 3

Informality and Profitability in Micro and Small Firms

This chapter presents the results of a new survey, carried out for this study, on the determinants of informality, and the effects of formality on the dimension of productivity related to profitability. The survey covers more than 600 micro, small, and medium enterprises in six Bolivian industries. We find that formality follows a continuum, moving from municipal licenses to tax number and very few small and micro firms are registered to other levels. A firm's decision to become formal is closely linked to the reason for going into self-employment, the ability of the entrepreneur to run its business, enforcement, and information costs related to formalization. Finally, the effect of formalization on profitability depends on the size of the firm.

We focus on firm profitability, rather than firm productivity, as our outcome of interest in the empirical analysis. There are several reasons for this choice. First, profitability is the measure of most importance to firm owners when deciding whether to become formal, regardless of whether formality increases profits through greater productivity, access to better input prices, economies of scale, or other channels. Second, since a large share of business's profits is withdrawn as income for the self-employed, profit is the measure of interest for considering poverty alleviation. Finally, there is a recent technical debate (see Katayama, Lu, and Tybout 2006) that suggests it can be very hard to measure the productivity of enterprises, especially using a single cross-section of data.

Simple comparisons of formal and informal firms reveal that formal firms are more productive. Fajnzylber, Maloney, and Rojas (2006a) estimate the impact of paying taxes and belonging to business associations on the performance of Mexican micro enterprises. They find relatively large impacts, with paying taxes estimated to increase business profits by at least 20 percent, and belonging to business associations estimated to increase business profits by at least 10 percent. Fajnzylber, Maloney, and Rojas (2006b), and Monteiro and Assunção (2006) investigate the impact of the Brazilian SIMPLES program. They find that firms that operate with a license have revenues at least 13 percent higher than informal firms, with much of this increase coming from a greater willingness of firms to operate out of fixed locations. Although they find some evidence of increased access to credit among formal firms, this does not account for much of the increase in revenues obtained by firms. A series of sector studies by the McKinsey Global Institute around the world comparing the operation of formal and informal firms concluded that informality has a very negative impact on productivity, even going so far as to conclude that "in Portugal and Turkey, for instance, informality accounts for nearly 50 percent of the overall productivity gap with the United States" (Farrell 2004).

Other studies do not show a significant impact of simplification efforts on registration of micro enterprises. Two recent studies on a business simplification program in Mexico give reason to be cautious about the likely effects of red tape reduction on the formalization of small firms. Although both studies find the program increased the number of registered businesses, they conclude that the new registered firms came either from wage workers entering self-employment (Bruhn 2006) or through the registration of larger informal firms with workers entering the social security system (Kaplan et al. 2006). Neither paper shows a large significant impact of the reform on registration among existing micro enterprises. This is consistent with the view that firms weigh the costs and benefits of becoming formal, and small firms see few benefits. Indeed, McKenzie and Woodruff (2006a) report that 76 percent of informal micro enterprises in their survey say the reason they are informal is that their business is too small, whereas only 10 percent of firms refer to the costs or time involved in registering.

However, such estimates ignore the fact that formality is a choice of firms; the lower productivity of informal firms may therefore just reflect less productive firms choosing to remain informal rather than be the consequence of informality. The identification strategy of Fajnzylber, Maloney, and Rojas (2006a) relies on assumptions about the formality status of firms being determined either on the basis of a set of observable variables or through a specific functional form in the estimation equation. If firms select into formality on the basis of unobserved owner ability or firm productivity, these may overestimate the impact of becoming formal. Given the questions that still exist as to the magnitude of any such effects, it is important to study how informality impacts on firms' productivity in the Bolivian context.

What Is the Level of Informality among the Surveyed Firms?

The formalization process of a firm in Bolivia can be accomplished through different steps that correspond to different degrees of formality. Box 3.1 summarizes the steps in the formalization process. Using these steps, we are able to summarize the degree to which firms are formal according to different dimensions of formality. In terms of legal definitions of formality, our survey asks firms whether they are registered with FundEmpresa, have a NIT, have a municipal license, and for those firms with workers, whether they have their workers registered with the CNS (health service), AFP (pension funds), and Labor Ministry (MT).

We find that formality follows a continuum, moving from municipal licenses to tax number and finally to FundEmpresa. Figure 3.1 illustrates the extent of overlap between the three main legal forms of business registration. We see that 44 percent of firms are completely informal, 28 percent having just a municipal license, only 2.5 percent having just a tax number, 21 percent having a tax number and municipal license, and 4 percent also having FundEmpresa. Less than 0.5 percent of firms have FundEmpresa without also having a tax number and municipal license. Thus, FundEmpresa appears to be the last step toward formalization for firms without workers. Registration of workers for health benefits, pension funds, and labor protections with the Labor Ministry are further steps toward full formality for firms with paid workers.[1] In light of the small number of firms registered with FundEmpresa and with CNS, AFP and MT, the rest of the chapter will focus on the two most common steps toward formality: registering for a municipal license and obtaining a tax number.

Box 3.1. The formalization process in Bolivia

---

1. Registering with FundEmpresa and getting a tax identification number (NIT) from the tax authorities Servicios de Impuestos Nacional (SIN). The two registration steps are not sequential in practice.

2. Operating with a license at the municipal level and at the state or sectoral level.

3. Registering your employees to the health benefits (Caja Nacional de Salud, or CNS), the social security (Administradoras de Fondos de Pensiones, or- AFPs), and to the Ministerio de Trabajo (Labor Ministry, or MT).

Formalization Process

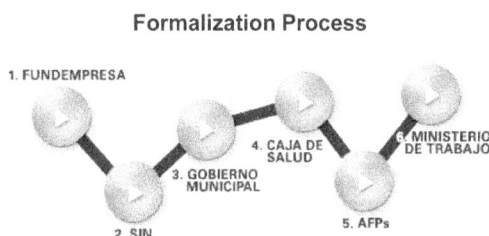

Source: www.tramites.gov.bo.

Figure 3.1. Share of firms at different degrees of formality

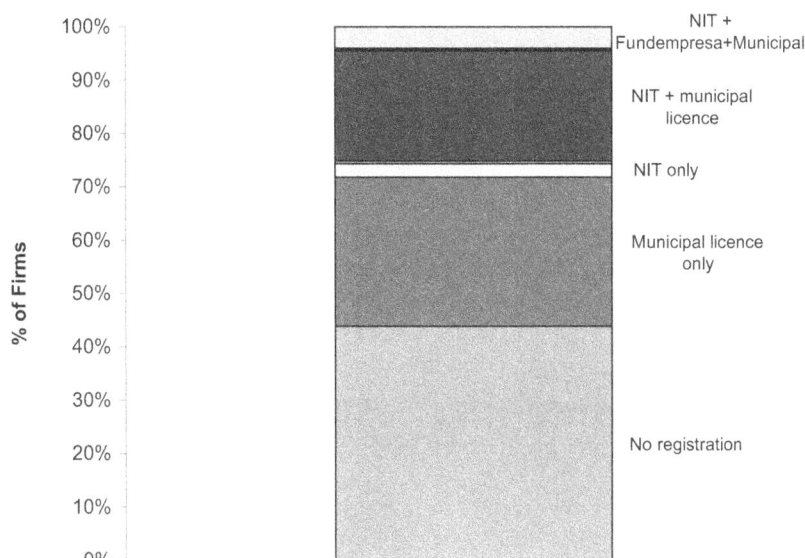

Source: Survey results.

The most common form of legal formalization is for a firm to have a municipal license. In our sample, 53 percent of firms have a license, 27 percent have a tax number, and only 5 percent are registered with FundEmpresa. The large majority of firms with paid workers (87 percent) have not registered a single worker with the national health insurance, a pension fund, or the Labor Ministry.

Additional evidence that registering for a municipal license is a first step toward formalization for some firms can be seen by examining when firms registered. Firms with a tax number and/or a municipal license were asked how long they had been in business at the time of registration (Table 3.1). Over two thirds of firms register at the time of start-up or within the first year, with only a 13–16 percent of registered firms registering after they had been in business for three or more years. If we look at the firms that have both a tax number and a municipal license, 66 percent got them both within the same year, 27 percent got the municipal license first, and 7 percent got their tax number first.

Table 3.1. Percentage of firms registering for tax identification numbers and municipal licenses, by the age of the firm at registration

Age of firm at registration	NIT	Municipal license
0 (registration when firm began)	56	59
Less than 1 year	12	15
1 to 2 years	16	13
3 to 4 years	5	5
5 or more years	11	8

Source: Survey results.

Other forms of formalization are not widely used. Other, less legalistic dimensions of formality include the extent to which firms keep accounts, the type of premises that businesses operate out of, the degree to which they use receipts, and whether or not they belong to industry associations or *sindicatos*. While two thirds of the firms keep some form of business records, only 28 percent use formal accounting services. One-third of the businesses operate in a fixed location outside of the household, with the rest either operating within their own dwelling, or in informal locations such as makeshift markets or directly selling on the street. Only 5 percent of firms say they always give a receipt with sales, with 13 percent of firms saying they give a receipt at least half of the time. These receipts can only be issued by firms with a tax number. However, depending on the tax regime of the issuer, the receipts may or may not be eligible for tax refunds.

Formality tends to be highest in the transportation, groceries, and food sales sectors and lowest in the camelid sector. Survey results by industry are given in Table 3.2. Membership in an association is strongest in the transportation sector, where firm owners say the benefit of membership is in protection of their route, and in helping them to negotiate with inspectors and the government.

Table 3.2. Percentage of formal firms, by dimensions of formality and by industry

	All firms	By Industry					
		Clothing	Transport	Groceries	Food sales	Wood	Camelids
Registered with FundEmpresa	5	6	11	4	3	4	2
Have a NIT	27	26	29	36	38	28	8
Have a municipal licence	53	46	63	75	61	61	12
Keep formal accounts	10	9	12	9	12	13	5
Keep some form of accounts	66	73	68	67	73	68	48
Always demand receipt for purchases	28	27	54	31	20	29	8
Always give receipt with sales	5	4	7	5	4	7	3
Give a receipt with sales at least 50%	13	11	13	16	14	21	3
Formal location outside dwelling	32	39	47	31	32	19	25
Belong to a sindicato or association	27	14	63	8	17	25	33
Firms with paid workers							
Worker registered with CNS (health)	10	7	10	16	8	13	4
Worker registered with AFP (pensions)	6	7	4	5	8	7	4
Worker registered with MT (labor)	8	10	11	11	8	6	4
Sample Size	629	101	112	103	107	100	106
Sample size with paid workers	379	70	72	38	72	82	45

Source: Survey results.

Formality is particularly low in rural areas. Our sample of wood and camelid firms is roughly split half and half between rural and urban locations. Only 10 percent of these firms in rural areas have a tax number, compared with 26 percent in urban areas, and no rural firms in our survey are registered with FundEmpresa. However, rural firms are only slightly less likely to have a municipal license than urban firms in the same industries. Firms in rural areas are farther away from the offices at which registration takes place, making registration more costly. In addition, they receive fewer visits from tax inspectors than urban firms. Only 20 percent of rural wood firms and 2 percent of rural camelid firms had received a visit from a tax inspector in 2006, compared with 41 percent of urban wood firms and 16 percent of urban camelid firms.

Formality increases with firm size, but even firms with 11 or more workers have low compliance in some dimensions. Figure 3.2 shows the percentage of firms complying with different legal aspects of formality, according to the number of workers they have. In our sample, no firm without workers is registered with FundEmpresa, compared with one-third of firms with 11 or more workers. For each firm size, we see that a municipal license is the most common form of formality, followed by a tax number. Worker registration is low among firms with 10 or fewer workers: less than 10 percent of these firms have a worker registered under any of the three types of worker registration. Even among firms with 11 or more workers, only half of them have workers registered.

Figure 3.2. Characteristics of formality, by firm size

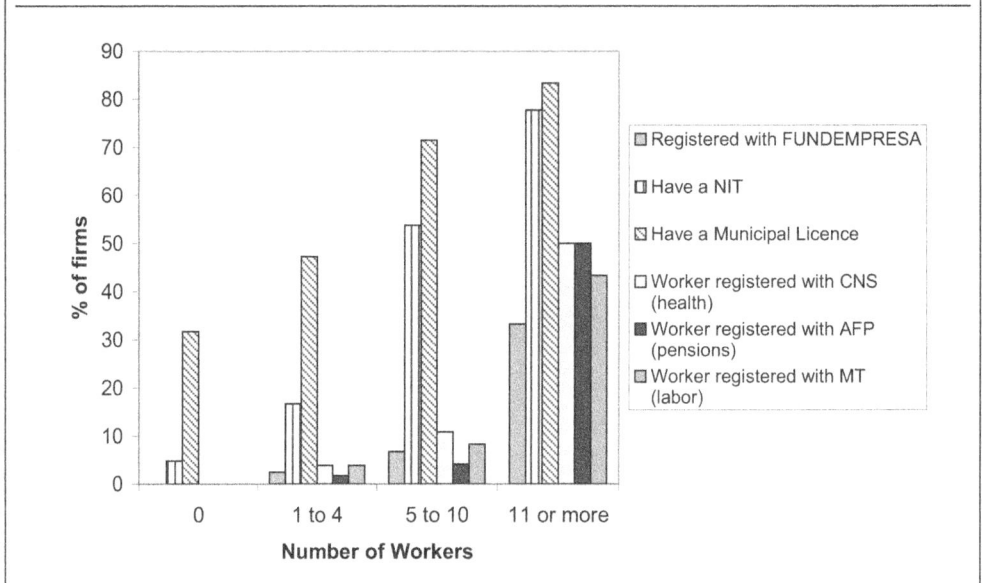

Source: Survey results.*Note*: Given that our survey only covers firms of size up to 25 employees, in some industries the distribution of firms registration to FundEmpresa, MT, CNS, may not match government figures.

Compliance is high with certain industry-specific legal requirements. In transportation, 97 percent of firms say that all their drivers have drivers' licenses, and 90 percent of transportation firms have their vehicles registered in the automobile registry. In the wood industry, two thirds of firms say that at least half the wood they use is certified, although only 22 percent say that 100 percent of the wood they use is certified. Our survey contains very few exporters: only 8 firms in wood and 15 in camelids. However, among these, only a minority belong to the chamber of exporters: 2 wood firms and 4 camelid firms. Given this small number of exporters, we cannot examine the impact of formality on the likelihood of exporting.

Which Firms Choose to Become Formal?

Firm owners will choose to become formal if the benefits from doing so outweigh the costs. We begin by examining what firm owners perceive as the benefits and costs, and then econometrically model the decision of a firm to formalize.

Costs and benefits of informality and formality

Firms report that the main benefit of having a tax number is to "obey the law," other benefits include increasing the number of customers and avoiding fines. Table 3.3 shows that almost half of the firms with a tax number say "obeying the law" is the main benefit. One quarter say that the main benefit is increasing the client base, through being able to cater to clients who need tax receipts, either for claims or for tax refunds. About 18 percent say the main benefit is avoiding fines, and 73 percent of firms with a tax number say they were visited by a tax inspector in 2006, compared with only 16 percent of firms without a tax number. Tax inspections are most common for firms in groceries and food sales—where 50 percent of firms received an inspection—and among larger firms: 61 percent of firms with five or more workers received an inspection, compared with 17 percent of firms with no workers and 20 percent of firms with one to four workers.

Table 3.3. Registered firms' perceptions of the main benefit of having a tax number and municipal license

	% of firms with NIT	% of firms with municipal license
Increasing client base	25	8
Avoiding fines	18	29
Reducing bribes	2	5
Better access to credit	2	2
Obeying the law	47	52
No benefit or don't know	6	5

Source: Survey results.

The main benefits of having a municipal license, according to registered firms, are to "obey the law" and to avoid fines. Between 66 and 70 percent of grocery and food sales firms report having been visited by a municipal inspector in 2006, confirming the view that municipal inspections are quite common in these sectors. Only 2 percent of firms say that better access to credit is the main benefit of being formal.

The few firms that are registered with FundEmpresa don't see much benefit from being registered. Some 39 percent of firms say they don't know of any benefit, while 45 percent say the main benefit is obeying the law and being legal. Hence, firms see FundEmpresa as an unnecessary step that they have to comply with (for instance to export or access government contracts) but that does not benefit them.

The majority of firms that are not registered with FundEmpresa have never heard of it and don't know what it does. Firms that did not have a tax number and firms not registered with FundEmpresa were asked the reasons for not registering. Only 11 percent of firms claim to know what FundEmpresa does, with a further 9 percent of firms saying they have heard of FundEmpresa but don't know what it does. Among the firms that claim to know what FundEmpresa is, but haven't registered, the main reasons given for not registering are that they don't see any benefit (38 percent) and they think their business is too small (48 percent).

Many firms also have limited knowledge about the process of getting a tax number. Almost half of all firms without a tax number (42 percent) say they don't know what a tax number is, and 35 percent say they don't know how to register. Only

40 percent of unregistered firms say they know where the nearest office of the Servicio de Impuestos Nacionales is. Other main reasons given for not having a tax number are that the business is too small (65 percent), the process is too time consuming (36 percent), and the costs of operating when registered are too high (33 percent).

Modeling the choice of firms to be formal

Firms will weigh the benefits and costs associated with formality and choose whether or not to register. The potential benefits of becoming formal are an increase in profitability as a result of higher productivity and better access to markets and to capital, freedom from fines levied against informal firms, harassment, petty corruption, and perhaps some moral or psychic benefit associated with compliance with the law. One interpretation of firms responding that the main benefit of formalizing is to obey the law is that this represents some moral or psychic benefit, although another interpretation is that it also represents less concern about inspections and fines being levied for noncompliance.

Costs of formalization include the money and time costs of registering, the tax costs involved for ongoing business, and the informational costs associated with learning about and deciphering complex registration procedures. Table 1.5 in Chapter 1 summarizes the time and money costs of registering, showing that on average it takes 23 days and costs Bs. 2,548 to fully register a unipersonal firm (although only 4 days and Bs. 2 to get a tax number). Median reported profits for firms in our sample are Bs. 815 per month, so this represents three months profits. The lack of knowledge about registration displayed by firms, shows that the informational costs of registration are also important. Finally, it is also likely to be easier for an informal firm to become formal than for a formal firm to try to become informal, so another cost of formalizing now is the loss of the option of changing formality status in the future.

Some costs of formalization are the same for all firms, but others depend on the size and nature of the firm. Although the monetary costs of registering are not variable, other costs will vary with the size of the firm (for example, taxes and the likelihood of enforcement), the ability of the firm owner, and the extent to which they hope to grow their business in the future. The probability that a firm will be formal according to a particular formality measure is then a function of the net benefit from registering, which we model simply as a function of owner, firm, sector, and location characteristics.[2]

Owner characteristics affect the decision to become formal not only through their effect on current and future profitability, but also through perceptions of the moral or psychic benefits of formality. Owner characteristics can also affect the degree to which credit constraints bind, which could also affect the decision to formalize given the lump-sum initial costs of formalizing. The owner characteristics we include are a combination of standard variables, such as gender, marital status, and education; family background variables, such as whether or not the owner spoke an indigenous language as a child, whether the owner's father owned a business, and a measure of how poor the individual was as a child;[3] and additional variables intended to measure the owner's ability and reasons for going into business. These variables include entrepreneurial self-efficacy (a combination of ability and self-confidence, see de Mel, McKenzie, and Woodruff 2007) and whether an individual says a very important reason for choosing self-employment over wage work was to care for family members along with work, to have flexible hours, and for the possibility of business growth. We would expect more able individuals who really want to grow their business to be more likely to become formal than individuals whose main reason for being in self-employment are nonpecuniary factors.

City and industry characteristics are also considered in analyzing the survey results. In addition to these owner characteristics, we add dummy variables for the city and industry. Enforcement is measured by the proportion of firms in the same city and industry that received inspections by tax inspectors in 2006. We expect that a firm is more likely to be formal (or feel the burden of informality) when firms in its industry and city are inspected regularly. Using geographic positioning (GPS) data on the location of the firm, we also control for the distance of the firm from the center of the city they are in or closest to. This is a proxy for access to markets. Fixed costs of registration are captured in the constant term, while costs of formality that vary with profitability are controlled for through the owner and firm determinants of profitability.

Firm size is likely to affect both the costs and benefits of being formal. Firm size might also be affected by whether the firm is formal: owners of informal firms may choose to stay relatively small to reduce the chances of detection, while larger formal firms may have grown large through reinvesting the extra profits arising from being formal. As a result, firm size is likely to be endogenous to the formality decision. We therefore model formality both with and without conditioning on firm size, where firm size is measured by the log of capital stock, excluding land and buildings, and by dummy variables for one to four workers, five to ten workers, and eleven or more workers.

Travel time and informational costs also affect formalization. Finally, we proxy the travel time and informational costs of registration with the distance of the firm from the government office where registration takes place. This is the Alcaldia office for municipal licenses, the Servicio de Impuestos Nacionales (SIN) office for tax numbers, and FundEmpresa office for FundEmpresa registration. Distance is measured using GPS coordinates of the firms and these offices, and is the straight-line distance. In a dense urban environment straight-line distances should provide a close approximation to travel distances (Gibson and McKenzie 2007). Annexes 3.1 and 3.2 provide the estimated marginal effects from this estimation. We summarize the results here.

Who holds municipal licenses? Municipal licenses are more common for more able entrepreneurs who have grocery stores, live close to the city center, and whose fathers owned businesses. Licenses are less common for individuals going into self-employment in order to be able to also care for children or parents and for firms in clothing and camelid industries. Municipal licenses are also less common in El Alto than in other cities. Firm size also is an extremely strong predictor of licensing: a firm with 11 or more workers is 37 percentage points more likely to have a license than a firm with no workers, while a firm at the 75th percentile of the capital stock distribution is 12 percentage points more likely to have a NIT than one at the 25th percentile. Other large magnitudes are:

- 14 to 16 percentage points lower likelihood of a municipal license for those in self-employment in order to be able to care for family
- 6 to 8 percentage points higher likelihood for someone at the 75th percentile of the entrepreneurial self-efficacy distribution compared with someone at the 25th percentile
- 8 to 10 percentage points higher likelihood for someone whose father owned a business
- 7 to 9 percentage points lower likelihood for a firm located 3.4 kilometers from the city center (the median) compared with a firm located right at the city center.

Who has a tax number? Tax numbers are more common for older, more able entrepreneurs, who went into self-employment for the prospect of business growth, face high tax inspection rates in their city and industry, and live close to the SIN office where registration takes place. Tax numbers are less common for individuals going into self-employment in order to be able to also care for children or parents and for firms in El Alto and La Paz compared with firms in Santa Cruz and Cochabamba. Controlling for these variables, there is no significant difference across industries. Again firm size is also an extremely strong predictor: a firm with 11 or more workers is 62 percentage points more likely to have a tax number than a firm with no workers, and a firm at the 75th percentile of the capital stock distribution is 12 percentage points more likely to have a license than one at the 25th percentile. Other large magnitudes are:

- 7 to 10 percentage points lower likelihood for those in self-employment in order to be able to care for family
- 6 to 9 percentage points higher likelihood for someone at the 75th percentile of the entrepreneurial self-efficacy distribution compared to someone at the 25th percentile
- 29 to 41 percentage points higher likelihood for a firm in a city and industry where 43 percent of firms receive a tax inspection (as is the case of groceries in Santa Cruz), the 75th percentile of the tax inspection distribution, compared to a firm in a city and industry where 14 percent of firms receive a tax inspection (such as Transport in El Alto), the 25th percentile
- 6 to 9 percentage points higher for individuals who went into self-employment for the prospect of business growth
- 11 to 14 percentage points lower likelihood for a firm 3.4 kilometers from the SIN office (the median distance) compared with a firm located right next to the SIN office.

Similar factors predict whether a firm with a municipal license also has a tax number. Older, more able owners, with high tax inspection rates, who live closer to the SIN office are more likely to have a tax number conditional on having a municipal license, as are larger firms. Camelid firms, which are less likely than firms in other sectors to get a municipal license, are more likely to get a tax number if they have a municipal license.

The small number of firms registered with FundEmpresa limits the extent to which we can model this registration decision. Larger firms and more able owners are more likely to be registered with FundEmpresa, but when we control for numerous characteristics simultaneously, no single characteristic is significant.

The decision to become formal does not significantly vary by gender, marital status, language as a child, poverty level as a child, or education level, conditional on these other characteristics. Women have a lower level of formality than men when we don't control for differences in characteristics: 22 percent of women have a tax number and 46 percent a municipal license, compared with 33 percent of men who have a tax number and 60 percent who have a municipal license. However, these differences can be explained by differences in the motivations for going into self-employment (women are more likely to value the ability to care for family), differences in self-efficacy (the women in our sample have lower entrepreneurial efficacy than men), and differences in the industries in which men and women are more concentrated. Likewise, while more educated individuals are more likely to be formal, the ability of the owner and reasons for being in business matter more than education alone for determining the choice to become formal.

Among bigger firms, some of the more able entrepreneurs may be opting out of formality because they don't see any benefit in it. We consider firms with workers and capital stock above the 75th percentile of our sample: that is, with more than five workers and with capital stock of Bs. 37,000 or more: 68 percent of these firms have a tax number, and 82 percent have a municipal license. When we model formality for these larger firms, we find that owners with higher levels of self-efficacy are less likely to have a municipal license or tax number, and additionally, entrepreneurs attracted to self-employment because of the chance of growing their business are less likely to have a tax number. Among these bigger owners without a tax number, 62 percent say that one reason for not having one is that they see no benefit in doing so. This contrasts with the smaller firms, where it is the more able entrepreneurs who are formal.

How Does Informality Affect Profitability?

Informal firms have low productivity and low profitability. In our survey, we see that the median monthly profits of firms with a tax number are Bs. 1,500, compared with Bs. 700 for firms without a tax number. However, it is less clear whether these lower profits are the consequence of informality or one of its causes. We therefore use the analysis in the previous section to model the choice to become formal and, based on this, estimate the impact of informality on firm profits.

We consider three approaches to measure the impact of formality on profitability. Our methods include (i) an ordinary least squares regression (OLS); (ii) a Treatment Effects regression that tries to take account of the potential endogeneity of formality; and (iii) an estimate using propensity score matching. See Annex 3.4 for the estimation methods and the choice of instruments to correct for endogeneity.

The impact of formality on profits

Results from the OLS regression show greater impact from obtaining a municipal license than a tax number. The increase in profits associated with formality drops as we control for more and more characteristics of the owner and firm (Figure 3.3 and Annex

3.3). When we just control for industry and location, firms with a tax number are found to have 65 percent higher profits, and firms with a municipal license 59 percent higher profits. Controlling for the gender, age, marital status, language, childhood poverty status, and education of the owner only narrows this gap slightly—down to 57 percent for those with tax numbers and 56 percent for those with municipal licenses. Our survey contains richer data on entrepreneurial ability than most surveys of micro enterprises. Controlling for these ability and motivation measures lowers the coefficient further, in accordance with the view that ability and formality are complements for the sample as a whole. However, even controlling for ability, we find profits to be 44–50 percent higher for formal firms. Controlling for the number of workers and capital stock lowers this difference more. After controlling for both these measures of firm size, firms with a tax number only earn 7 percent higher profits, and we cannot reject the possibility that there is no difference in profitability from firms without tax numbers. However, firms with a municipal license still earn 25 percent more than firms without a municipal license, even after controlling for firm size. However, if we compare OLS regressions for the effect of a tax number on profitability for larger firms, controlling for industry, city, and owner characteristics, but not owner ability, we find profits are 63 percent *lower* for the bigger firms with a tax number than for the bigger firms without one. This difference drops to 39 percent lower profits once we control for owner ability, with the small sample preventing us from being able to reject the possibility that the difference is zero. This is in accordance with the view discussed above that formality and ability are *substitutes* for larger firms in our sample.

Figure 3.3. Percentage difference in profitability of formal and informal firms after controlling for different observable characteristics

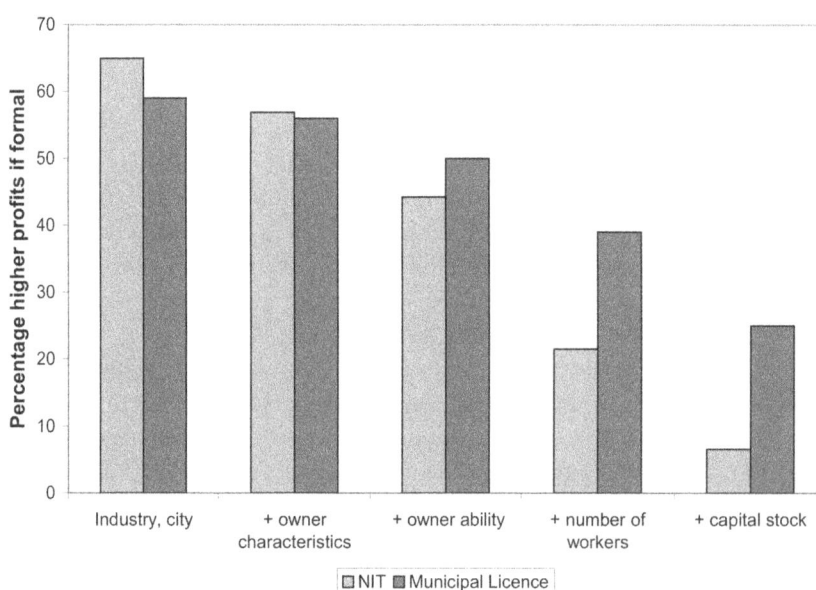

Source: Results from the OLS regressions.

Propensity-score matching estimates show larger gains in profits from formality, even after matching on firm size. Table 3.4 summarizes the estimated average treatment effects for different dimensions of formality. Having a tax number is associated with 58 percent higher profits, which drops to 36 percent higher once we match on firm size. Having a municipal license is associated with 50 percent higher profits, dropping to 37 percent higher once we condition on firm size. If we examine the effect of having a municipal license without a tax number, and a tax number with a municipal license, we also find higher profits. This suggests that both dimensions of formality have value for firms. Finally, we examine one potential channel through which having a tax number might boost profits by comparing the treatment effect of having a tax number and giving tax receipts to that of having a tax number and not giving tax receipts. The gain in profits is much higher when firms also give tax receipts. This is in accordance with the perception of firms that a main benefit of having a tax number is to allow them to increase the customer base through issuing tax receipts.

We also find a substantial increase in profits from having a tax number when we use distance to the SIN office as an instrument for formality. Profits are estimated to be 60 percent higher for firms with a tax number when we do not control for firm size, and 74 percent higher after controlling for firm size.[4] The results when we do not condition on firm size are similar to the propensity score matching estimates, providing us with some confidence that the propensity score estimates for other dimensions of formality are also reliable.

The most likely explanation for the difference in these estimates is that there is heterogeneity across firms in the effect of formality. Heterogeneity would lead each of the different estimation methods to pick up the treatment effect for a different set of firms. With heterogeneous treatment effects, the maximum-likelihood estimate is what is known as a local average treatment effect. Intuitively, it describes the effect of obtaining a tax number for a firm whose formality is affected by its closeness to the SIN office. Such firms are likely to be those that would benefit from formality, but for which the information or time costs of registering are too high. Hence we would expect these firms to have greater benefit from a tax number than the average firm.

Table 3.4. Percentage increase in profits associated with different dimensions of formality, by firm size

	Without matching on firm size	Matching on firm size
Having a NIT	58***	36***
Having a NIT conditional on having a municipal license	39***	27*
Having a municipal license	50***	37***
Having a municipal license conditional on not having a NIT	42***	32***
Having a NIT and giving receipts vs no NIT	98***	81***
Having a NIT and not giving receipts vs no NIT	40***	22

Source: Results from the propensity score matching.
Note: *, **, and *** indicate significance at the 10%, 5%, and 1% levels respectively. Estimation is conditional on being within 10 kilometers of the registration office.

Furthermore, the propensity score treatment effect is comparing the average difference in profits for very similar formal and informal firms. Thus it is picking up the effect of formalizing for firms at the cusp of becoming formal. Again, such firms may have more positive effects for formality than firms that are far from becoming formal. For example, the fact that we see a tax number in only 10 out of the 138 firms with capital stock below Bs. 1,550 (the 25th percentile), suggests there are few benefits to having a tax number for very small firms.

Further propensity score matching analysis suggests that the benefits of holding a tax number are greatest for mid-size firms. To examine the effect for firm size further, we carry out propensity score matching estimates of the effect of a tax number according to firm size. The results (see figure in Box 3.2), while not showing significant differences, offer suggestive evidence to support the view that the benefits of a tax number are greatest for neither the smallest nor the largest firms in our sample.

Box 3.2. Getting a NIT pays off for small firms, but not for the micro or medium-size firms in our sample

The box figure (below) shows that having a NIT increases profits for firms with two to five workers and capital stock of Bs. 8,000–34,000, but decreases profits for firms who become formal at smaller sizes and for informal firms who become formal at larger sizes.

Average impact of having a tax number on profitability, by firm size

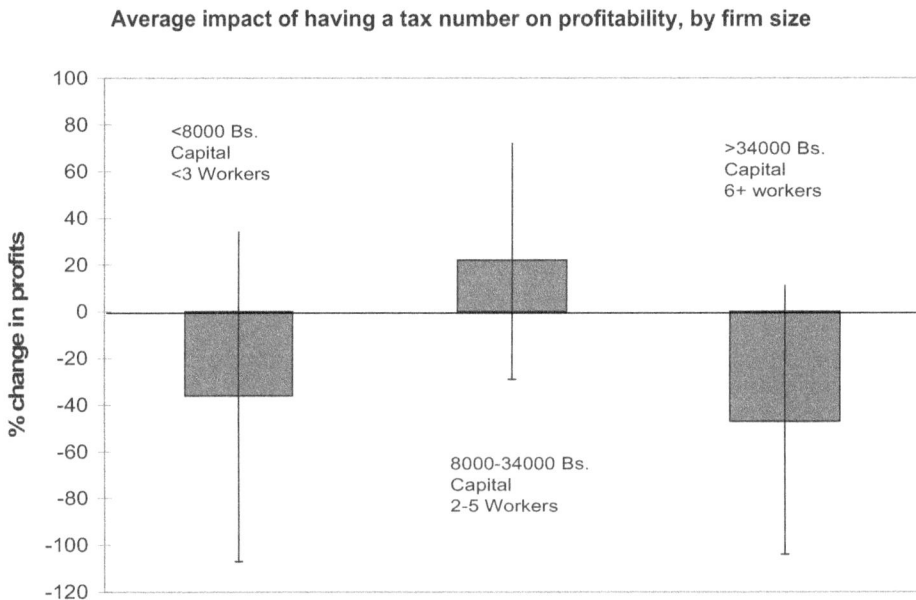

Note: Bars show point estimates from propensity score matching. Lines show 95 percent confidence intervals.

(Box continues on next page)

Box 3.2 (continued)

What explains the nonlinear relationship seen in the above figure? Firms of different sizes face different costs and benefits of becoming formal:

- The smallest firms don't immediately benefit from becoming formal. Formalizing immediately involves more costs, but these firms are too small to benefit from increased customer base or better access to credit. However, if these firms plan on growing over time, this current cost of formalizing can be justified in terms of the benefits awaiting them as they become slightly bigger. For this reason, we find that firm owners who formalize when small tend to have higher entrepreneurial ability and more plans for business growth.

- Firms who wait and formalize when they are in the middle size group (two to five workers and Bs. 8,000–34,000) are now big enough to enjoy some immediate benefits from formalizing. Section IV of this chapter shows the main benefit of getting a NIT appears to be the ability of a firm to expand its customer base by issuing tax receipts.

- Firms in our sample which have managed to get to a larger size—six or more workers and above Bs. 34,000 in capital stock—face a fall in profits from formalizing. These larger informal firms tend to have owners with less formal education, but higher entrepreneurial ability than firms of the same size with a NIT. Only 28 percent of them report receiving a visit from a tax inspector in the last year, compared to 81 percent of formal firms their size. Although we find these larger informal firms are less likely to get trade credit than formal firms of their size, we find that they are just as likely to have received loans, and are more likely to have received working capital, from banks or other financial institutions as formal firms with the same size. Thus for a firm which has managed to reach this size while staying informal, the main impact of getting a NIT is just higher taxes.

These larger informal firms are not completely informal. In particular, 71 percent of them have a municipal license, even though they do not have a NIT. It is thus likely that the municipal license is allowing them to be formal in the eyes of the municipal authorities, and possibly with financial institutions, even though they are not registered with the tax authorities. This suggests that for these larger firms, it is not that there are no benefits of formality, but rather than there are no additional benefits from a NIT once a firm has a municipal license.

Source: Survey results.

For firms with less than the median capital stock and number of workers, the effect of having a tax number is estimated to be 36 percent *lower* profits (with a standard error, or s.e., of 35 percent); for firms with capital stock and number of workers between the median and 75th percentile, having a tax number is estimated to increase profits by 22 percent (s.e., 26 percent); while for firms with above the 75th percentile for capital stock and workers, having a tax number is estimated to lower profits by 47 percent (s.e., 29 percent).

There are clear differences in the effect of becoming formal for different types of firms. Typically firms in the middle range of the sample, see benefits from formalizing. It is not surprising that there is unlikely to be any benefit of formalizing for very small firms, since even if they are formal, they may be unlikely to be given credit or receive new customers, and just face the costs of formalizing. It is perhaps more surprising that the larger firms in our sample of small and medium enterprises don't appear to have any benefit from formalizing. As discussed previously, informal firms that get to this size are typically owned by high-ability individuals, who are likely to have succeeded in obtaining financing and customers in order to get the firm to the size it is. Formalizing may therefore confer little benefit in this regard, but instead subject the firm to additional costs. Box 3.3 presents findings on gender differences in informality and profitability.

Box 3.3. Gender differences in formality and profitability

Female entrepreneurs in our sample are less likely to be formal: 60 percent of male owners have a municipal license compared to 46 percent of female owners; 33 percent of male owners have a NIT compared to 22 percent of female owners; and only 1.6 percent of female owners are registered with FundEmpresa, compared with 8.3 percent of male owners. Female owners also earn lower profits on average: mean (median) monthly profits are Bs. 1,202 (Bs. 566) for female owners compared to Bs. 2,127 (Bs. 1,000) for male owners.

However, when we estimate the probit equation examining determinants of formality separately for men and women, the size and sign of most coefficients are fairly similar. In a pooled probit with interactions between each characteristic and a female dummy variable, we can't reject joint insignificance of all the interactions. That is, we can't reject that the determinants of formality are the same for men and women.

Similarly, when we examine the impact of a NIT and other characteristics on profitability, we can not reject that formality has the same impact on male-owned businesses as it does on female-owned businesses. Moreover, again we can not reject that a full set of interactions between the owner characteristics and a female dummy are jointly zero, so that the production function producing profits is the same for men and women. Hence, all things being equal, men and women behave the same way; however, all things are not equal, which causes the lower formality and lower profits for female entrepreneurs.

Our analysis suggests four main factors that explain the lower formality and lower profits of female entrepreneurs in our sample:

1. Differences in the reasons for entering business. 75 percent of females say that the ability to care for family members is a very important reason for going into self-employment, compared to 47 percent of males. Going into self-employment for this reason is associated with lower formality and lower profits, as business growth is not the prime focus of such businesses.

2. Differences in education and ability. Females in our sample are less likely to have post-secondary education, and display lower levels of entrepreneurial ability (measured by self-efficacy), even conditional on education. More able entrepreneurs are more likely to be formal and earn higher profits.

3. Female businesses tend to be smaller in size than male businesses; and larger businesses are more likely to be formal and earn higher profits.

4. Female enterprises are concentrated in different sectors from male enterprises: Females are more likely to be involved in food sales, camelid products, and groceries, and less likely to be in transport and wood. Female businesses are twice as likely to be operated out of the home as male businesses, which is associated with a lower likelihood of visits from tax inspectors. However, the greater tendency to work out of home is a function of the industry they work in—controlling for industry of work, females and males are equally likely to work at home.

Source: Survey results.

The return to capital

The OLS and maximum-likelihood estimates give an estimated monthly return to capital in the 12 to 14 percent range (see Columns 5 and 7 of Appendix 3.3). However, the return to capital is likely to decline with the level of capital stock: McKenzie and Woodruff (2006b) find a return of approximately 10 to 15 percent per month for Mexican firms with less than US$500 in capital stock, dropping to 1–2 percent per month for firms with US$1,000 to $5,000 in capital. Estimating the return separately over these ranges, we find a monthly return of 12 percent for firms with US$50 to $500 of capital stock, and a return of 2.3 percent per month for firms with US$1,000 to $5,000 of capital stock. The mean interest rate for firms receiving loans is 2.1 percent per month in our sample. Smaller firms can easily cover this interest rate with their expected return on capital, whereas firms with larger amounts of capital stock may find themselves operating at a level where their return on capital equals the market interest rate: that is, at their optimal size given the financial market.

What Are Some of the Channels through which Formality Increases Profits?

The previous section has found evidence that having a municipal license and a tax number increases profitability, at least for some firms. As discussed in Chapter 2, there are several channels through which formality might improve profitability. Our survey allows us to examine some of the more important channels: (i) the access to credit and financial services; (ii) the size of the customer base; (iii) the extent of mark-ups; (iv) the payment of taxes; (v) the perceived obstacles to business growth; and (vi) the use of technology. Each is discussed below.

Impact on access to credit and use of financial services

Being registered with the tax authorities appears to have no significant impact on a firm's access to credit. The only marginally significant effect we see is on use of a savings account, which is more common among registered firms. We examine the impact of having a tax number on various measures of use of financial services, including whether the firm receives trade credit, has had working capital or loans from banks, has a saving account, and participates in PASANAKU (a ROSCA-type alternative to formal financing). We find no significant effect of having a NIT on access to trade credit, bank credit, or overall finance use.

One possible reason for finding no impact of formality on access to credit is that few firms of any type use the financial system. Table 3.5 summarizes the percentage of firms that use different types of financial instruments. It is not the case that no firms use the financial system, but only a minority of firms does. Firms with four or fewer workers are particularly likely not to use the financial system much. One potential reason for this is lack of availability of services: 65 percent of our grocery and food sale firms say there is no bank branch within five blocks of their business. However, another reason could be lack of demand at the going market prices, particularly among the larger firms not using credit. Given the high return to capital found for smaller firms, the low use of loans, trade credit, and working capital among these firms suggests a lack of access to credit at the going market interest of 2 percent per month for these firms. The issue of access to credit for very small firms seems to be driven less by price effects than by quantity. Small firms' returns on capital suggest that they could afford the going interest rates and could benefit from borrowing at this rate. However, they do not get the credit. Either they are discouraged by the requisites or the lack of flexibility from financial institutions, which cause them not to apply, or financial institutions ration the supply of credit to this segment because they deem the business too risky or costly.

Table 3.5. Percentage of firms using different types of financial instruments, by firm size

		Number of workers			
	All	0	1 to 4	5 to 10	11 or more
Trade credit	16	12	15	20	24
Bank credit for start-up	26	19	25	33	12
Working capital from Banks	20	21	19	20	29
Savings account	26	12	22	39	65
Loan from financial institution in 2005 or 2006	31	14	31	39	47
Plays pasanaku	17	15	17	19	18
Business accepts cheques	10	0	7	16	53
Business accepts credit cards	1	0	0	4	12

Impact on the customer base

One of the main benefits of having a tax number, according to the firms themselves, is the ability to give tax receipts, allowing them to increase their customer base. Indeed, in Table 3.5 we saw that, after matching on firm size, firms with a tax number that don't give tax receipts benefit from having the tax number only one quarter as much as firms with a tax number that also give receipts. This increase in customers is not coming through more contracting with the government, multinationals, or large firms: 97.3 percent of our firms make no sales to any of these entities. Further evidence of more customers is seen through questions that ask firms how often they have no customers. Grocery firms with a tax number are 19 percentage points less likely to have many periods during the day without customers than firms without a tax number, controlling for firm size and firm and owner characteristics. Transport firms with a tax number spend a larger share of each day with customers and less time idle.

Impact on mark-ups

Another potential way that formal firm owners may be able to increase profits is by increasing the mark-up received per customer. This could occur through access to cheaper input prices or by charging higher output prices. To avoid concerns about possible differences in quality of products between formal and informal firms, we examine this question only for grocery stores, where we can consider homogenous products across firms. We asked firms the price at which they purchase and sell ten common items (e.g., a 2-litre bottle of Coca Cola, a tin of San Lucas sardines, a 1-litre bag of PIL milk). We find firms with tax numbers have marginally lower mark-ups than firms without tax numbers for eight out of the ten products, although in all but one case, the difference is not significant. Likewise we find no systematic differences in the output or input prices for these goods. Thus it does not appear that formal firms are charging higher prices.

Impact of formality on payment of taxes

In addition to these potential benefits, formality also involves costs. The clearest cost of having a tax number is paying business taxes. We find firms with a tax number are 37 percentage points more likely to pay taxes than firms without a tax number, and with the amount of additional tax paid equivalent to 11 percent of profits. Even conditional on paying some business taxes, we find firms with a tax number pay a 12 percent higher share of their profits than firms without a tax number. This cost occurs for both smaller and larger registered firms in our sample: firms with capital stock above the 75th percentile pay higher taxes equivalent to 8–18 percent of profits if they have a tax number.

Impact of formality on perceived obstacles to business growth

Firms in the sample that have formalized by getting a tax number or municipal license are less likely than informal firms to regard corruption and access to credit as business obstacles. To examine other potential channels through which formality might lead to higher profitability of the firm, we carry out probit regressions for the extent to which a firm perceives different factors as obstacles to the growth of their business, conditional on owner and firm characteristics. The main findings from this exercise are:

- Firms with a tax number are more likely to view taxes, labor force training, and labor law as main obstacles to the growth of their firm and less likely to view corruption as a major constraint to firm growth.
- Firms with a municipal license are less likely to view the requirements of accessing credit, the cost of credit, contracts enforcement, and customs and trade regulations as major constraints to firm growth.

This provides some suggestive evidence of other channels through which formality might be influencing profitability: in particular, less corruption for firms with a tax number, and lower costs of credit and contract enforcement for firms with a municipal license.

Impact on use of technology

Formal firms may be more likely to use new technology. This could occur if new technology becomes worth investing in because the firm's customer base is expanding, because formality allows additional access to credit, and/or because formality makes it easier to rent technological equipment. We carry out propensity score matching to investigate the impact of a tax number on technology use by comparing firms with similar owner and firm characteristics in an industry, matching also on the value of log capital stock. The main results are as follows:

- Grocery firms with a tax number are significantly more likely to use freezers, digital balances, and telephones.
- Food sales firms with a tax number are significantly more likely to use industrial ovens, freezers, digital balances, cash registers, and telephones.

- Wood firms with a tax number are significantly more likely to use joint-fingers and *cepilladoras*.
- We do not find higher use of technology among formal firms in the camelid, transportation, and clothing industries.

Conclusions

The specialized survey of micro, small, and medium enterprises used in this study has allowed us to examine the different dimensions of formality in Bolivia. Our findings shed light on the determinants of the decision of a firm to become formal, the consequences of this decision for profits, and some of the potential channels through which profits are affected. The main conclusions are:

- Formality follows a continuum, moving from municipal licenses to tax numbers and finally to FundEmpresa registration.
- Lack of knowledge is a barrier to formalization. Few firms have knowledge of FundEmpresa or its purpose, and many are also ignorant about the process of obtaining a tax number.
- Among micro and small firms, it is the more able entrepreneurs who are formal. Formality is also closely linked to the reason for going into self-employment.
- Both enforcement and information costs are strong determinants of the decision to get a tax number. Firms in industries and cities with high inspection rates are more likely to register, while those who operate their business further away from the SIN office are less likely.
- Among the larger firms in our sample, the firms that remain informal tend to be operated by more able entrepreneurs, who see little benefit in formalizing.
- Both a municipal license and a tax number are found to increase profits for the average firm formalizing. The increase in profits from a tax number is much larger for firms that also give receipts than for firms that don't give receipts.
- However, the very small and the largest firms in our sample may see lower profits from becoming formal.
- The increase in profits from a tax number appears in large part due to increasing the customer base related to the fact that formal firms can issue receipts that are tax deductible. It does not come from higher mark-ups, lower input prices, or better access to credit. Firms with a tax number also view corruption as less of an obstacle, suggesting a reduction in bribes. However, they pay more taxes and are more likely to view labor laws as constraints to further business growth.

Annex 3.1. What is the scope of the new survey?

A new survey undertaken for this study investigates the determinants and impacts of informality at a microeconomic level among micro, small, and medium enterprises. We carried out surveys of 629 firms in six industries during March 2007.[5] The industries chosen for the survey were grocery stores, restaurants and food sales, manufacturing of clothing from wool and cloth, transportation of passengers and cargo, manufacturing of clothing from camelid wool (from llama and alpaca), and manufacturing of furniture from wood. In each industry except transport we survey a mix of micro firms with less than five workers (including self-employed with nonsalaried workers) and small firms with 5–20 workers. In transport, the sample was divided into passenger and cargo transport, and further by type of transport; in this sector some firms were medium-size (having more than 20 workers).

Industries were chosen to represent a large portion of the active population, to encompass a diversity of formal and informal sectors, and to include both urban and rural firms. The 2005 MECOVI survey[6] shows that the most common urban industries of the self-employed and employers are retail trade (18 percent), construction (11 percent), transport of cargo and passengers (10 percent), preparation and sale of food (5.6 percent), and manufacture and sale of clothing (3.3 percent). We therefore have four of the top five industries for urban small and medium enterprises.[7] We then chose two industries linked to Bolivia's agriculture sector, for which we could survey in both urban and rural areas. The choice of camelids and wood was made on the basis of these being industries with some export activity, which the government has designated as priority sectors (*complejos productivos*).

The survey sampled both urban and rural firms. Surveying was carried out by the Bolivian survey firm Encuestas & Estudios. Sampling in the urban areas of La Paz, El Alto, Cochabamba, and Santa Cruz was done using a geographic information database maintained by the survey firm. This database is based on a census of all economic establishments in these cities carried out in August 2005 and includes enterprises operating within households. In addition, a census of people selling items on the street was carried out in La Paz/El Alto during late 2004 and early 2005, providing supplementary information. In addition, for the transport sector, a census of all firms that have registered their cars was used. Using this information, the survey is able to provide a reasonably comprehensive sampling frame in urban areas. Less information was available for constructing a sampling frame in rural areas. Therefore, to sample camelids and wood, the survey firm used a "snowball" technique to populate the sample in rural areas. A total of 2,402 firms were interviewed, of which 629 were used in the final sample, indicating a high refusal rate, probably related to the difficulty of interviewing informal firms. The detailed composition of the data by size, sector, and city is given in Table 3.A.3.1.

Table 3.A.3.1. Survey sample by size, sector, and city

	La Paz	Santa Cruz	Cochabamba	El Alto
Grocery stores				
Small firm	12	14	8	10
Micro firm	19	16	13	11
Total	31	30	21	21
Restaurants and food joints				
Small firm	10	13	6	7
Micro firm	10	10	6	7
Comideras	12	10	8	8
Total	32	31	20	22
Textile clothing				
Fabric				
Small firm	6	8	6	5
Micro firm	12	13	11	5
Wool				
Small firm	4	0	1	4
Micro firm	8	9	3	6
Total	30	30	21	20
Transport				
Taxis	10	10	10	6
Radio taxis	3	3	3	3
Colectivos	2	2	2	2
Omnibuses, Micros	8	7	7	10
Departamental	2	2	2	
Provincial	2	2	2	
Total	27	26	26	21
Camelid clothing				
Urban				
Small firm	4	0	3	3
Micro firm	16	0	7	18
Rural				
Small firm	1	0	0	3
Micro firm	19	15	5	12
Total	40	15	15	36
Manufacturing of wood products				
Urban				
Small firm	3	10	6	1
Micro firm	4	10	10	7
Rural				
Small firm	4	11	6	0
Micro firm	4	9	8	7
Total	15	40	30	15

Annex 3.2. Personal, geographic, and industry characteristics of entrepreneurs holding municipal licenses and tax numbers

Marginal results from Probit estimation

	Municipal Licence				NIT			
	(1)	(2)	(3)	(4)	(5)	(6)	(7)	(8)
Female	-0.0650	-0.0657	-0.0458	-0.00991	-0.0569	-0.0752	-0.0348	0.0216
	(0.065)	(0.065)	(0.068)	(0.074)	(0.047)	(0.048)	(0.047)	(0.039)
Age of owner	0.00373	0.00390*	0.00416*	0.00299	0.00375**	0.00380**	0.00418***	0.00352***
	(0.0023)	(0.0022)	(0.0023)	(0.0024)	(0.0017)	(0.0017)	(0.0016)	(0.0013)
Married	0.0666	0.0666	0.0693	0.0778	0.0367	0.0281	0.000725	-0.00742
	(0.053)	(0.053)	(0.054)	(0.057)	(0.039)	(0.039)	(0.040)	(0.033)
Indigenous language as kid	-0.0123	-0.00263	-0.0300	-0.0482	-0.0239	-0.00762	-0.0464	-0.0219
	(0.063)	(0.062)	(0.063)	(0.067)	(0.046)	(0.047)	(0.043)	(0.035)
Has post secondary edn	0.0330	0.0213	0.000709	0.0146	0.0753	0.0516	0.0318	0.00910
	(0.059)	(0.059)	(0.061)	(0.065)	(0.046)	(0.045)	(0.043)	(0.034)
Basic edn or less	0.00786	0.0181	0.0328	0.0631	-0.0626	-0.0536	-0.0384	-0.0319
	(0.071)	(0.070)	(0.072)	(0.076)	(0.050)	(0.050)	(0.049)	(0.038)
Entrepreneurial Self-efficacy	0.0257*	0.0255*	0.0207	0.0208	0.0269***	0.0249**	0.0184*	0.0125
	(0.014)	(0.014)	(0.014)	(0.015)	(0.010)	(0.010)	(0.010)	(0.0084)
Reason for s/e is carer for kids/parents	-0.139**	-0.134**	-0.144***	-0.161***	-0.0974**	-0.0752*	-0.0823*	-0.0201
	(0.055)	(0.055)	(0.055)	(0.060)	(0.044)	(0.043)	(0.042)	(0.034)
Reason for s/e is flexible hours for housework	0.0488	0.0487	0.0727	0.0912	-0.0113	-0.0257	-0.000654	-0.0259
	(0.053)	(0.053)	(0.054)	(0.057)	(0.040)	(0.040)	(0.038)	(0.033)
Reason for s/e is prospect of business growth	0.0443	0.0409	0.0107	-0.00948	0.0928**	0.0884**	0.0619*	0.0237
	(0.054)	(0.053)	(0.055)	(0.058)	(0.037)	(0.036)	(0.036)	(0.031)
Father owned a business	0.0983*	0.0934*	0.0882	0.0795	0.0375	0.0446	0.0234	-0.00884
	(0.053)	(0.053)	(0.054)	(0.057)	(0.042)	(0.041)	(0.040)	(0.031)
Average tax inspection rate at city*industry level	0.263	0.254	0.0555	-0.0710	0.708**	0.939***	0.785***	0.674***
	(0.38)	(0.38)	(0.39)	(0.41)	(0.28)	(0.29)	(0.29)	(0.24)
El Alto	-0.147**	-0.136*	-0.0998	-0.0317	-0.112**	-0.137***	-0.0995**	-0.0411
	(0.074)	(0.074)	(0.077)	(0.083)	(0.045)	(0.043)	(0.044)	(0.040)
La Paz	-0.0960	-0.0805	-0.0385	0.0651	-0.114**	-0.133***	-0.0892*	-0.0351
	(0.090)	(0.090)	(0.092)	(0.098)	(0.055)	(0.051)	(0.053)	(0.047)
Cochabamba	0.00864	0.0192	0.0249	0.113	0.00883	-0.0587	-0.0452	-0.0187
	(0.084)	(0.084)	(0.086)	(0.089)	(0.060)	(0.054)	(0.053)	(0.043)
Food	-0.173**	-0.169**	-0.251***	-0.256***	0.0448	0.0162	-0.0790*	-0.0276
	(0.078)	(0.078)	(0.078)	(0.083)	(0.063)	(0.059)	(0.045)	(0.042)
Clothing	-0.350***	-0.343***	-0.445***	-0.464***	-0.0178	-0.00720	-0.110**	-0.0524
	(0.084)	(0.085)	(0.074)	(0.073)	(0.077)	(0.079)	(0.052)	(0.048)
Wood	-0.229**	-0.215*	-0.363***	-0.417***	0.00479	0.0679	-0.0825	-0.0521
	(0.11)	(0.11)	(0.099)	(0.092)	(0.084)	(0.095)	(0.063)	(0.049)
Camelids	-0.526***	-0.521***	-0.598***	-0.598***	0.0847	0.215	0.0840	0.111
	(0.097)	(0.099)	(0.075)	(0.070)	(0.17)	(0.20)	(0.18)	(0.17)
Transport	-0.155	-0.150	-0.255*	-0.376***	0.101	0.183	0.115	0.0733
	(0.15)	(0.15)	(0.14)	(0.12)	(0.13)	(0.15)	(0.14)	(0.12)
Log distance to city centre	-0.0616*	-0.0597*	-0.0672*	-0.0691*	-0.0530***	0.0546*	0.0664**	0.0418
	(0.036)	(0.036)	(0.037)	(0.040)	(0.015)	(0.030)	(0.030)	(0.026)
Child poverty index		-0.0119	-0.00665	-0.00108		-0.00893	-0.00475	-0.00236
		(0.021)	(0.021)	(0.023)		(0.015)	(0.015)	(0.012)
Log distance to Alcaldia office	0.0252	0.0247	0.0520	0.0684				
	(0.037)	(0.037)	(0.039)	(0.042)				
Log distance to SIN office						-0.121***	-0.119***	-0.0927***
						(0.029)	(0.029)	(0.024)
One to Four workers			0.202***	0.166***			0.204***	0.155***
			(0.056)	(0.061)			(0.049)	(0.046)
Five to Ten workers			0.291***	0.231***			0.521***	0.413***
			(0.067)	(0.082)			(0.078)	(0.097)
Eleven or more workers			0.433***	0.368***			0.686***	0.616***
			(0.071)	(0.12)			(0.12)	(0.19)
log capital stock				0.0435***				0.0444***
				(0.016)				(0.010)
Observations	557	557	557	499	557	557	557	499

Standard errors in parentheses, *** p<0.01, ** p<0.05, * p<0.1

Omitted dummy variables for industry and city are groceries and Santa Cruz.

Annex 3.3. Personal, geographic, and industry characteristics of entrepreneurs who hold municipal licenses and have registered with FundEmpresa or obtained tax numbers

Marginal results from Probit estimation

	Fundempresa				NIT given that have municipal	
	(1)	(2)	(3)	(4)	(5)	(6)
Female	-0.00823	-0.00650	-0.00428	-0.00529	-0.118	0.0655
	(0.0080)	(0.0065)	(0.0045)	(0.0065)	(0.084)	(0.11)
Age of owner	0.000522*	0.000425	0.000250	0.000172	0.00520*	0.00655*
	(0.00031)	(0.00027)	(0.00020)	(0.00018)	(0.0030)	(0.0036)
Married	-0.00424	-0.00337	-0.00344	-0.00503	0.0319	0.0208
	(0.0071)	(0.0055)	(0.0043)	(0.0056)	(0.073)	(0.087)
Indigenous language as kid	-0.00312	-0.00133	-0.00254	-0.00314	0.0260	0.00781
	(0.0060)	(0.0046)	(0.0029)	(0.0038)	(0.085)	(0.099)
Has post secondary edn	0.0227	0.0157	0.00940	0.00414	0.0671	-0.00257
	(0.015)	(0.012)	(0.0085)	(0.0055)	(0.075)	(0.087)
Basic edn or less	0.0000500	0.00153	0.000851	0.00212	-0.102	-0.103
	(0.0095)	(0.0081)	(0.0048)	(0.0060)	(0.094)	(0.11)
Entrepreneurial Self-efficacy	0.00393*	0.00290	0.00154	0.00109	0.0342*	0.0429*
	(0.0021)	(0.0019)	(0.0013)	(0.0011)	(0.019)	(0.022)
Reason for s/e is carer for kids/parents	-0.00557	-0.00275	-0.000898	0.000217	-0.0674	0.00163
	(0.0072)	(0.0051)	(0.0027)	(0.0019)	(0.075)	(0.091)
Reason for s/e is flexible hours for housework	-0.00272	-0.00306	-0.000971	0.000178	-0.0757	-0.123
	(0.0061)	(0.0049)	(0.0027)	(0.0020)	(0.075)	(0.096)
Reason for s/e is prospect of business growth	0.00200	0.00230	0.00148	0.00113	0.146**	0.0619
	(0.0051)	(0.0038)	(0.0023)	(0.0020)	(0.070)	(0.085)
Father owned a business	-0.000609	0.000808	0.000274	0.000245	0.0978	0.0131
	(0.0053)	(0.0043)	(0.0025)	(0.0020)	(0.073)	(0.088)
Average tax inspection rate at city*industry level	0.00115	0.00649	-0.00812	-0.00299	1.058**	1.462**
	(0.046)	(0.034)	(0.021)	(0.016)	(0.52)	(0.59)
El Alto	0.0237	0.0260	0.0238	0.0102	-0.165*	-0.0339
	(0.021)	(0.022)	(0.021)	(0.014)	(0.093)	(0.13)
La Paz	-0.00342	-0.000227	0.00184	0.00114	-0.196*	-0.0765
	(0.0086)	(0.0079)	(0.0064)	(0.0047)	(0.11)	(0.14)
Cochabamba	0.00719	0.00571	0.00517	0.00360	-0.0470	-0.0440
	(0.013)	(0.011)	(0.0092)	(0.0078)	(0.11)	(0.12)
Food	0.00221	0.0000119	-0.00289	-0.00230	0.108	0.0224
	(0.012)	(0.0078)	(0.0031)	(0.0029)	(0.099)	(0.12)
Clothing	0.00447	0.00713	-0.00224	-0.00144	-0.0207	-0.0385
	(0.020)	(0.020)	(0.0036)	(0.0028)	(0.15)	(0.17)
Wood	-0.00319	0.000938	-0.00290	-0.00198	0.0688	-0.0935
	(0.011)	(0.012)	(0.0037)	(0.0030)	(0.15)	(0.16)
Camelids	0.0207	0.0221	0.00102	0.00138	0.375*	0.502**
	(0.060)	(0.060)	(0.012)	(0.012)	(0.23)	(0.21)
Transport	0.0193	0.0284	0.00712	0.00820	0.150	0.195
	(0.046)	(0.057)	(0.023)	(0.028)	(0.20)	(0.24)
Log distance to city centre	-0.00237	0.00594	0.00398	0.00191	0.0665	0.0644
	(0.0025)	(0.0056)	(0.0040)	(0.0027)	(0.052)	(0.065)
Child poverty index		-0.00389	-0.00171	-0.00132	0.00544	0.00237
		(0.0026)	(0.0016)	(0.0016)	(0.027)	(0.031)
Log distance to SIN office					-0.137***	-0.140**
					(0.051)	(0.061)
log distance to Fundempresa		-0.00760	-0.00463	-0.00259		
		(0.0056)	(0.0042)	(0.0031)		
One to Four workers			0.000188	-0.000696		0.357***
			(0.0029)	(0.0022)		(0.094)
Five to Ten workers			0.0258	0.0244		0.551***
			(0.025)	(0.026)		(0.095)
Eleven or more workers			0.0530			0.565***
			(0.069)			(0.10)
log capital stock				-0.000773		0.0859***
				(0.00094)		(0.029)
Observations	557	557	557	499	290	251

Standard errors in parentheses, *** p<0.01, ** p<0.05, * p<0.1
Omitted dummy variables for industry and city are groceries and Santa Cruz.

Annex 3.4. Estimation methods

We consider three approaches to measure the impact of formality on profitability. Our methods include (i) an ordinary least squares regression (OLS); (ii) a Treatment Effects regression that tries to take account of the potential endogeneity of formality; and (iii) an estimate using propensity score matching.

Methodology for the OLS regression

The ordinary least squares regression is based on the following equation:

$$\ln\left(PROFITS\right)_i = \lambda + \alpha Firms'Characteristics_i + \beta Owners'Characteristics$$
$$+ \gamma Industry_i + \delta Location_i + \theta Formal_i + \varepsilon_i.$$

The outcome of interest here is θ, which measures the average increase in log profits associated with being formal, conditional on the other variables included in the regression. Assigning a causal interpretation to formality based on this estimation requires assuming selection on the observable variables included in this equation, as well as assuming that the linear functional form adequately captures profits.

A key concern with OLS estimation of equation (2) is that the error term ε is correlated with formality. There are several possible reasons for this concern. First, if we exclude firm size from (2), we would expect a positive bias, due to larger firms earning higher profits and also being more likely to be formal. In the OLS results we should therefore expect the estimate of θ to become less positive as we include firm size. Second, a concern is that ε may include unmeasured ability of the firm, with higher ability leading to more profits and also affecting the decision to become formal. If ability is a complement to formality, we should again expect this to lead to an upward bias in θ. This is what we found among smaller firms. However, among larger firms there appeared to be a negative relationship between (measured) ability and formality. For these firms, ability may be a substitute for formality. Able owners may have no trouble attracting customers and financing and perhaps are also more successful at avoiding fines. Thus, among larger firms we might expect a downward bias in θ. The overall bias when we pool firms is therefore unclear.

Methodology for the Treatment Effects regression

A second approach to estimation is to try and take account of the potential endogeneity of formality by instrumenting for formality status when estimating (2). Since formality is a binary variable, we use STATA's treatreg command to fit a maximum-likelihood Treatment Effects model. The instrument we rely on is the distance from the firm to the location of the office where the firm would have to register. As shown in the previous section, distance to the SIN office strongly predicts whether a firm has a tax number.[8] However, distance to the Alcaldia office is not a strong predictor of whether a firm has a municipal license, conditional on the other variables included in this regression. A possible reason for this is that the municipality is more active in both disseminating information about how to register and also in enforcement. In contrast, many firms lack information about where the SIN office is or how to get a tax number. Thus we can only use this Treatment Effects model for modeling the impact of a tax number, not the impact of a municipal license.

The *t*-statistic on log distance to the SIN office is around 3.8, after conditioning on the other variables in the regression. If we restrict to firms within 10 kilometers of the SIN office, this drops to 3.5, which is still strong and significant. Thus, this distance instrument provides a strong first stage.

The exclusion restriction we rely on here is that, conditional on the distance of a firm to the city center, and the average tax enforcement in a firm's city and industry pair, distance to the SIN office has no direct impact on profitability. One possible reason this assumption could be violated would be if firms choose where to operate with the location of the SIN office in mind. However, as previously discussed, a majority of firms do not know where the SIN office is, and many firms operate out of their homes. Within a large city it seems that the location of the tax office is not a main concern when deciding where to locate.

Methodology for the propensity score matching

Finally, to complement the OLS and Treatment Effects regressions, we also provide estimates of the impact of being formal on profits using propensity score matching. Propensity score matching assumes that all selection occurs on observables, but does not require assuming a linear function form. Additionally, use of propensity score matching allows us to estimate the impact of a municipal license, for which we do not have an instrumental variable. We use the same variables as in the OLS regressions, along with higher-order interaction terms in carrying out the match.

Annex 3.5. Impact of a tax number on log profits

| | OLS Regression | | | | | Maximum-likelihood | |
	(1)	(2)	(3)	(4)	(5)	(6)	(7)
NIT	0.649	0.569	0.442	0.215	0.066	0.597	0.744
	(5.62)**	(4.94)**	(3.90)**	(1.89)	(0.58)	(1.50)	(2.73)**
log distance to city	-0.047	-0.034	-0.064	-0.039	-0.014	-0.058	0.002
	(1.46)	(1.04)	(1.97)*	(1.18)	(0.44)	(1.63)	(0.05)
Average tax inspections	-2.183	-2.006	-1.423	-1.717	-1.644	-1.572	-2.182
	(3.03)**	(2.80)**	(2.13)*	(2.65)**	(2.56)*	(2.02)*	(3.17)**
Female		-0.441	-0.332	-0.262	-0.121	-0.321	-0.115
		(3.45)**	(2.56)*	(2.14)*	(1.02)	(2.61)**	(0.94)
Age		-0.004	-0.005	-0.003	-0.003	-0.005	-0.004
		(0.89)	(1.25)	(0.71)	(0.68)	(1.29)	(0.94)
Married		0.070	0.106	0.075	0.115	-0.130	0.012
		(0.71)	(1.09)	(0.82)	(1.24)	(1.21)	(0.12)
Young firm		-0.113	-0.147	-0.102	-0.042	0.095	0.077
		(1.04)	(1.38)	(0.99)	(0.42)	(0.94)	(0.80)
Indigenous language as kid		0.069	0.107	0.020	0.116	0.106	0.126
		(0.50)	(0.82)	(0.15)	(0.90)	(0.94)	(1.13)
Has post secondary edn		0.129	0.169	0.155	0.141	0.158	0.131
		(1.16)	(1.52)	(1.45)	(1.37)	(1.42)	(1.22)
Basic edn or less		0.070	0.045	0.075	0.110	0.054	0.137
		(0.52)	(0.34)	(0.59)	(0.87)	(0.43)	(1.14)
Child poverty		-0.088	-0.079	-0.072	-0.063	-0.078	-0.064
		(2.33)*	(2.12)*	(1.98)*	(1.83)	(2.04)*	(1.69)
Entrepreneurial Self-efficacy			0.108	0.096	0.090	0.103	0.075
			(4.22)**	(3.91)**	(3.79)**	(3.63)**	(3.03)**
Reason for s/e is carer			-0.247	-0.245	-0.230	-0.240	-0.216
for kids/parents			(2.40)*	(2.53)*	(2.36)*	(2.35)*	(2.19)*
Reason for s/e is flexible			-0.021	0.008	0.052	-0.022	0.032
hours for housework			(0.22)	(0.08)	(0.55)	(0.23)	(0.34)
Reason for s/e is prospect			0.103	0.062	0.057	0.090	0.025
of business growth			(1.04)	(0.65)	(0.60)	(0.89)	(0.27)
Father owned a business			-0.210	-0.193	-0.269	-0.210	-0.257
			(2.17)*	(2.05)*	(2.91)**	(2.16)*	(2.69)**
One to four workers				0.232	0.142		0.047
				(2.05)*	(1.24)		(0.44)
Five to ten workers				0.894	0.712		0.506
				(6.26)**	(4.76)**		(3.02)**
Eleven or more workers				1.050	0.885		0.529
				(3.39)**	(3.18)**		(1.65)
Log capital stock					0.139		0.115
					(4.76)**		(4.37)**
Constant	7.447	7.690	7.616	7.287	5.939	7.630	6.291
	(31.06)**	(23.02)**	(23.17)**	(22.24)**	(14.42)**	(22.77)**	(14.77)**
Observations	492	488	488	488	447	488	447
R-squared	0.22	0.26	0.32	0.38	0.43		

Robust t statistics in parentheses, * significant at 5%; ** significant at 1%

Table 3.A.5.1. Impact of a tax number on access to credit and use of financial services

	Trade Credit			Bank credit for start-up			Working capital from Banks		
	(1)	(2)	(3)	(4)	(5)	(6)	(7)	(8)	(9)
NIT	0.150	0.078	0.089	0.031	-0.003	-0.019	-0.020	-0.030	-0.078
	2.94***	0.57	0.84	0.52	0.02	0.13	0.64	0.18	0.60
Size controls	no	no	yes	no	no	yes	no	no	yes
Method	probit	treatreg	treatreg	probit	treatreg	treatreg	probit	treatreg	treatreg

	Savings Account			Loan from Bank in 2005/06			Plays Pasanaku		
	(10)	(11)	(12)	(13)	(14)	(15)	(16)	(17)	(18)
NIT	0.096	0.236	0.164	0.056	0.043	0.020	-0.013	-0.119	-0.128
	1.74*	1.64*	1.38	0.93	0.25	0.14	0.29	1.14	1.22
Size controls	no	no	yes	no	no	yes	no	no	yes
Method	probit	treatreg	treatreg	probit	treatreg	treatreg	probit	treatreg	treatreg

	Overall finance use		
NIT	0.369	0.391	0.210
	2.30*	0.68	0.50
Size controls	no	no	yes
Method	ols	treatreg	treatreg

Note: NIT indicates the holding of a tax number; treatreg indicates maximum-likelihood Treatment Effects regression.

Notes

[1] Principal components analysis suggests that registration with CNS, AFP and MT involves more formality than registration with FundEmpresa (which in turn is more formal than just a NIT or municipal license).

[2] In particular, we estimate the following probit equation for the likelihood of a firm's being formal, as defined by having a municipal license, having a tax number, and being registered with FundEmpresa:

$$\Pr(Formal = 1) = \lambda + \alpha Firms'Characteristics + \beta Owners'Characteristic + \gamma Industry + \delta Location + \eta Enforcement + \varepsilon$$

[3] Child poverty is formed as a principal component of the frequency with which the individual skipped meals as a child, the education of the child's mother, and the type of floor in he child's dwelling. It is intended to proxy long-term family wealth before the operation of the current business.

[4] The difference between the estimate of 60 percent higher and 74 percent higher is not significant. One explanation for the point estimate increasing is nonlinear effects of formality by firm size (see discussion below).

[5] The regressions dropped firms where the owner was not the one interviewed (since we need owner characteristics) — this accounts for 65 firms. The regressions also dropped firms with more than 25 employees, which accounts for 12 firms. At the end the regressions included 557 firms out of the 629 interviewed.

[6] MECOVI is an acronym for the Spanish form of Living Standards Measurement Survey.

[7] We did not survey construction, since it was felt there was little overlap between very small informal firms and large formal firms; and because the broad industry grouping is quite heterogeneous, including skilled engineers and architects as well as less skilled workers.

[8] Further evidence for the validity of the assumption that distance to the SIN office is picking up information about getting a NIT rather than some general location characteristic affecting the incentives for formality is seen in the fact that distance to the SIN office does not significantly predict which firms get a municipal license or register with FundEmpresa.

CHAPTER 4

Policy Recommendations

This chapter draws on the fresh findings of the previous chapters regarding firms decision to become formal, the effect of formality of firms profits, and the constraints to higher productivity to recommend policies to increase the formalization, profitability, and productivity for micro and small firms in Bolivia. In this context, the recommendations support the objective of the PND to increase productivity and provide incentives for the formalization of micro and small firms. Reducing Bolivia's very high level of informality is critical to raise economic growth and sustain it over the long term. Informality limits the productivity and growth of firms and thus reduces the potential growth of the economy; reduces tax revenues despite continuing to make use of costly public services; weakens social protection for the labor force, increasing the burden on government social protection programs; and undermines both public and private institutions by promoting lack of respect for the law, corruption, and weak contract enforcement.

The recommendations below focus on two broad areas: (i) increasing the formalization of micro and small firms; and (ii) taking actions to promote productivity growth among all micro and small firms. The first section presents policy recommendations to increase the formalization of micro and small firms through increasing the benefits of becoming and remaining formal, increasing information about formalization; reducing the complexity and cost of licensing, registration and tax procedures. That section also considers ways to increase the impact of formality on profitability, given the finding that the economic benefits of formality depend significantly on the size of the firm. The second section recommends measures to increase the productivity of micro and small firms in Bolivia by removing operational constraints on access to financial, physical, and human capital and by easing institutional and regulatory constraints. The third section presents the current strategy and actions undertaken by the government.

The impact of formalization on profitability should guide the focus of government actions. Formalization has a significant positive impact on the profitability of small firms, which have reached an optimal size to enjoy the benefits of formality and can internalize those benefits in their production to set the basis for future growth. As a result, policies toward this group of firms should be to increase information regarding the formalization process and the benefits of formality, and to help reduce the administrative and regulatory complexity and cost of formality. For micro firms, the costs of formalization are too large and hence do not translate into benefits, therefore policies for this sector should be oriented more toward promoting productivity and growth, such that they can start reaping the benefits of formality as they grow. For the largest firms, which have succeeded in reaching their size without being formal, stricter enforcement of formalization requirements may be the most effective measure.

Government actions to promote formalization can thus cover a wide range of incentives and enforcement measures. Some of the principal policy and practice recommendations for reducing the regulatory and administrative barriers to formalization are summarized in Box 4.1.

Box 4.1. Policy and practice recommendations for reducing regulatory and administrative barriers to formalization

1. Develop a commonly shared toolkit that encompasses the full range of successful donor informal economy interventions.

2. Promote formalization by creating a regulatory environment that is generally enabling.

3. At the same time, work with willing partners to remove barriers to enterprise growth and formalization at local level. Wholesale legal reform is not always possible, but progress can still be made to streamline administration (as through one-stop shops).

4. Support measures to reduce corruption at the main interfaces between government and business in the process of formalization (particularly in registration and licensing procedures).

5. Educate government officials at local and national levels about the importance of the informal economy and the role they can play in increasing formalization through offering improved services. Demonstrate that facilitating long-term growth of the tax base is preferable to extracting short-term gains and encouraging firms to hide their activities.

6. Ensure that programs to increase welfare in the informal economy do not reduce incentives to formalize. In return for assistance, require a quid pro quo from informal enterprises in terms of movement towards formalization.

7. Support dialogue between government and informal enterprises (or their associations) to reveal barriers to formalization and build trust and understanding on both sides.

8. Consider the merits of longer interventions, because reforming regulatory and administrative barriers and the culture of government takes time. Where longer interventions are not possible, adopt more modest and targeted objectives.

9. Assess the capacity of local governments to implement policies to reduce barriers to formalization, and take steps to plug gaps between centrally approved initiatives and local capacities.

10. Undertake and share further research on the impact of enabling environment reform on formalization.

Source: USAID 2005.

What Can Be Done to Increase the Formalization of Micro and Small Firms?

Policy recommendations must take account of the reasons micro and small firms choose to remain informal or to become formal identified in the previous chapter. Firms base their decisions on becoming formal on a variety of factors: (i) the need for flexibility and independence to fulfill family obligations; (ii) high cost and complexity of procedures; (iii) lax government enforcement; (iv) distance to tax office; and (v) self-efficacy of the individual entrepreneur (a mix of entrepreneurial ability and self-confidence). To increase formalization, policies have to address two kinds of factors:

those that make the benefits of formalizing small and those that make the costs of formalizing high. Policy measures discussed below are grouped into four areas, in order of timing and priority: increasing information on the processes and benefits of formalization, reducing the cost and complexity of licensing, taxation and registration procedures to become formal, increasing the incentives to become formal, and improving enforcement.

The recommended sequencing of policy changes includes both short- and long-term actions. In the short term, priorities are to improve information about formalization and increase the benefits of formalization and the costs of remaining informal. In the medium term, simplifying and reducing taxes payments for micro and small firms are both critical actions. Working to increase the benefits of formalization and improving enforcement are secondary medium-term priorities. In the longer term, actions should be designed to increase the transparency about the use of taxes collected, so as to change how people view the state and how they regard their responsibility to pay a fair share of services they receive.

Information

Increasing information can encourage the formalization of micro and small firms quickly and at a relatively low cost. Many informal firms interviewed in the focus groups did not even know what it meant to be formal or what the national business registry FundEmpresa was. Worse, some firms thought they were formal when they were not (transport firms, for example). Therefore, improving information about formalization—particularly by publicizing how firms become formal, what they can gain by becoming formal and what they risk by staying informal—has the potential to increase awareness and encourage the first step for formalization. The information strategy could cover the following aspects:

- *Why does it matter to be formal?* Firms should be aware that formality can help them grow their business through different channels, including access to more clients, to credit, to government contracts, to subcontracting, and to government or donor-funded training programs. In contrast, staying informal has costs related to corruption, being illegal, risking fines, not growing or achieving economies of scale, and ultimately not succeeding in business.

- *How do you become formal?* Firms should have information about the role and location of the municipal registry, FundEmpresa, the tax authorities (SIN), the health authority (CNS), pension funds (AFPs), and the Labor Ministry (MT). In particular, the usefulness of the different steps to become formal should be reassessed. In the case of FundEmpresa, 39 percent of those registered with it did not know any benefit from being registered with them. The registration process should be smoothed out and simplified for firms (see below), and the different registries should be better coordinated at different levels of government. One option would be to have a one-stop shop that covers municipal and central requirements, which would need to be carefully designed to work well. Examples from many countries around the world, for example Indonesia and Egypt, could be useful in this regard.

How is the tax money used? Firms paying taxes to the central or the municipal government should have some knowledge about how that money is spent. Simplified information on the National Development Plan and the objectives of sectoral policies would create a space for citizen participation and monitoring. Policies to improve transparency can be linked with the current project on monitoring and evaluating public expenditure. This can be reinforced with publications describing government spending, as well as e-government tools, fixed information centers and mobile units that can reach firms through more innovative ways. Television and radiocast could also be used to disseminate information.

Mechanisms to disseminate information on formalization are critical, but they should be separate from enforcement mechanisms. All this information can be disseminated through information centers, as is done in the United Kingdom, or mobile systems to reach out to people even in rural areas like radiocasts. The municipalities are better at enforcing compliance, hence they are better known. However, it is advisable that the information body be separated from the enforcement body, so that firms can be more open to the information provided and trust the benefits of formalization offered.

Incentives to formality

Policy actions should aim to increase the benefits of formalization and the costs of remaining informal. Benefits of formalization can consist of linking registration with access to more clients to formal firms. Several possibilities exist to make this link, including easier access to export markets, government contracts, clustering initiatives, or subcontracts with larger firms. Other options include offering registered firms access to training for workers, improved access to finance, reduction of taxes, and simplification of other procedures. Interventions may be bundled, as in Peru which linked access to collateral (through titling), credit, and business training. Other kinds of incentives—such as allowing firms to issue receipts and improving access to financing, markets, and training—could also encourage formalization. Evidence shows that being able to issue receipts is a major benefit of formalization, because it expanded the customer base. Hence, public policies to enable even firms in the simplified regimes to issue receipts can be beneficial. From the focus group analysis, access to finance was the main constraint to productivity, so initiatives to link registration with an improved access to finance could be beneficial.

Building self-efficacy creates a crucial change in attitudes among firm owners that tends toward formalization. Increasing the self-efficacy of entrepreneurs, so that they get into business to grow their business, significantly increased formalization. Policy could be geared toward building the self-efficacy of entrepreneurs through training and developing small business associations, which create a space for sharing ideas and mentoring with other successful entrepreneurs. Poorly designed government entrepreneurship training would be a concern; hence the need to carefully craft any public intervention (Box 4.2).

Box 4.2 The role of training and business associations in raising the self-efficacy of informal entrepreneurs

---

Karlan and Valdivia (2006) show that providing entrepreneurial training alongside credit positively impacts the economic outcomes for both women entrepreneurs and micro-credit institutions. Using a randomized control trial, the authors measure the marginal impact of teaching basic business skills to Peruvian women entrepreneurs enrolled in the group lending program FINCA. They find that training improves business knowledge, practices and revenues for the women entrepreneurs, and leads to higher repayment and client retention rates for the lending institution. Strengthening women's formal or informal systems of organizing, networking and information sharing is a second way to bridge the capability gap between men and women.

The example of the Self-Employed Women's Association (SEWA) in India is a prime case of the successful organization of self-employed women. Founded by a trade union organizer in 1972 as a union of women workers in the informal economy, SEWA had to spend over two years to be registered as a trade union, over ten years to be recognized by some of the International Trade Secretariats, over 20 years to be invited to join the National Labor Congress of India, and 30 years to be invited to be an official member of the worker delegation from India to the International Labor Conference. In trying to gain official recognition within the international labor movement, SEWA has served as an inspiration for three other international movements: the women's movement, the micro-finance movement, and a growing movement of informal workers and producers.

Source: Chen and Carr (2004).

Simplify licensing, registration, and taxation procedures

International programs to simplify firms' registration procedures and reduce tax payment have proved effective in increasing formalization. Results from Brazil's SIMPLES program—which simplified firms' registration procedures and reduced tax payment (up to 8 percent) for eligible micro and small firms—and Mexico's SARE program—which reduced firms' registration procedures to three days—have both been found to have a limited positive impact in promoting formalization and firm creation. For a greater impact, such simplification programs need to be strongly tied with benefits to become formal (Box 4.3). The impact of administrative simplification programs may be larger when accompanied by other complementary measures aimed, first, at increasing the potential benefits of joining the formal sector—e.g., facilitating access to credit or government provided technical assistance—or, second, at reducing other costs of regulatory compliance, beyond the facilitation of firm registration. The challenge is to distinguish relevant from anachronistic regulations and balance private costs and legitimate public interests, such as the protection of public safety or the environment. Improving the simplified tax regime for micro and small enterprises is also an essential component to incentivize formalization. Because so few micro and small companies now pay any business taxes, reducing the simplified tax regime to a minimal level probably would prove to be a net gain for both the fiscal accounts and for formalization. It can also be noted that when the enforceability of regulations is related to the size of the firm, as is the case in Bolivia, supporting economic packages in favor of micro and small informal firms, without a prior enhancement of the regulatory environment, may only increase the number of micro and small firms, generate temporal abnormal profits in existing firms without having any effect on their growth, and imply a long term transfer to informal-market consumers (Giugale and El-Diwany 1997).

Enforcement

Policies should also be designed to increase enforcement, so as to increase the cost of remaining informal; however they should not be targeted to smaller firms and should always be accompanied with incentives. Many informal firms in the focus group interviews reported that inspections were irregular, loose, and only conducted around peak periods, such as holidays. Firms in the focus group in transport reported lax enforcement; in camelids the situation was similar. It seems that larger firms were more subject to inspections and control, and petty corruption was involved. Indeed, based on the 2006 ICA, small firms report that corruption is an important constraint to their development. Hence, cracking down on enforcement has to be accompanied by anticorruption measures. For tax enforcement at the national level, this means reaching out to rural areas and to firms far from a local tax office and being more systematic in inspections. Enforcement may be made more efficient by decentralizing tax offices to get closer to their constituency. However, Chapter 3 showed that smaller firms should not be the primary target of enforcement as it would increase their costs of doing business. Enforcement should be accompanied by incentives to be an effective tool to formalize larger firms.

Box 4.3. Goals when reducing barriers to formalization

Best Practice in Reducing Barriers to Formalization
Summary of Recommendation for Donor Intervention

- Support broad programs of regulatory reform to simplify new and existing laws and make the business climate more hospitable to formal enterprise. Introduce Regulatory Impact Assessment.
- Simplify official administration for businesses. Review and reduce paperwork.
- Design measures to create a business-friendly culture in government and improve the quality, quantity, and accessibility of services. Consider service charters and one-stop-shops for business.
- Simplify tax administration; consider singe taxes for MSMEs.
- Avoid retroactive taxation for enterprises that formalize.
- Share information on what tax revenues are used for, and how businesses will benefit from enhanced services.
- Rationalize business registration and licensing regimes, and separate the one from the other. Use IT to streamline the process and share information.
- Separate the function of revenue generation from business registration.
- Restrict licensing to those activities where it is justified on health, safety, environmental, consumer protection, or other grounds.
- Reduce registration fees and statutory requirements, e.g. for fixed premises, capital.
- Identify areas for labor law reform, protecting essential rights while making it easier to hire and fire workers and to employ on flexible contracts.
- Make it easier to register producer associations so that the benefits of formalization can be made available to groups comprising individuals who would not separately have made the effort to formalize.

Source: USAID 2005.

What Can Be Done to Increase Productivity of Micro and Small Firms?

The main operational constraints to higher productivity shared by all sectors are related to access to physical, financial, and human capital. Additional constraints identified in the focus group surveys were the lack of public policies to promote research and technology diffusion (camelid), the lack of standards and quality control to step up production at a larger scale (wood), the lack of marketing strategies to support exports with trade agreements and positioning in potential markets. Institutional and regulatory constraints to higher productivity are related to tax rates, business licensing and registration of firms, corruption, and macroeconomic and political instability. The following policy recommendations are drawn from international experience to address each of the constraints mentioned. Because of the additional social constraints faced by women entrepreneurs, a special section is included here on policy recommendations to help meet their needs.

Increasing access to finance

Improving credit information, especially coordinating among all regulated financial institutions, has a great potential to decrease the informational costs of providing credit to micro and small firms. Sharing credit information allows financial institutions to acquire information about the credit history of loan applicants and hence identify the risk characteristics of their applicants. Without that information, banks are likely to ration credit to new firms or to demand higher interest rates. Because the cost of acquiring information about an applicant is fixed, a bank would rather invest in acquiring information about larger firms than micro or small firms. Therefore, government should continue encouraging private and public credit registries and the promotion of credit scoring information to lower lenders' costs of providing credit to micro and small firms. In addition, the information sharing should allow micro and small firms to borrow from banks as well as *microfinancieras*.

A strong creditors' rights environment, as well as the use of collateral, can help micro and small firms' access credit at lower cost. Pledging collateral allows the lending institution to reduce the asymmetric information regarding the borrower and the project, and thus reduce moral hazard. However, the legal environment should enable the lender to seize the collateral at low costs in case of default. If lenders feel that regulations do not protect them and their chances of repossessing the collateral are too low, they might ask for more collateral (increasing the cost of credit) or ration credit for many borrowers (decreasing the amount of credit lent). In the case of informal firms where the property rights on the collateral may not be clear, the role of the creditors' rights framework and collateral to mitigate credit risk is even greater. Policy measures to improve collateral use and creditor rights include streamlining laws on collateral collection and increasing the agility of the judicial system regarding bankruptcy proceedings, as well as designing innovative ways to use collateral for micro and small businesses, such as the use of moveable rather than only fixed assets.

Loan guarantee schemes have proved successful in increasing access to finance for small firms. The approach entails bringing into the credit relationship a guarantee from an agent that has privileged information on the borrower or the project. For instance, a large firm can guarantee credit for its supplier (reciprocal loan guarantees), as it can impose an extra cost on the supplier if it defaults. This is particularly useful when the enforcement of credit contract environment is weak. In Argentina, nearly 4,000 small and medium enterprises have benefited from this type of scheme to get a loan. The government, too, through a public agency can be the partial guarantor of a loan given by a group of financial institutions to firms in a certain region, industry, or size. Banks pay a fee to obtain the guarantee instead of insurance in case of default. FOGAPE in Chile and FNG in Colombia have been particularly successful in efficiently channeling resources to micro and small firms. The main implementation challenge for such schemes is how to allow banks to alleviate risk. In addition banks do not have to "provision" for lending to firms without collateral, as required by the regulation. Hence, there is still a moral hazard, but on the part of the bank. One way to deal with that would be that the fee allocated to the bank be a function of the bank's history of default (IDB 2005).

Credit subsidies or directed lending through development banks have channeled financing to micro, small, and medium firms around the world. In the Republic of Korea, Nugent and Yhee (2002) report that small and medium enterprises benefited substantially from subsidized credit. In Brazil, the National Economic and Social Development Bank (BNDES), the largest development bank in Latin America, financed nearly 100,000 operations for micro and small firms in 2003. The principle is that by lowering interest rate costs of firms, firms can afford the loan, and they become less prone to default (hence less risky). However, the success and sustainability depend on the details like the level of competition among banks, as a bank can still find a way to pass the subsidy to other–than-intended firms in that case. Kumar and Francisco (2004) establish that large firms benefit more from BNDES than small firms, according to data from the Investment Climate Assessment. Another risk is attached to the distortion in the competition with other financial institutions that are working with micro and small firms like *microfinancieras*—which in Bolivia are world-class. The implementation challenge is that such an announcement raises many expectations from the public. The size of the subsidy, as well as the channel of the subsidy, should be carefully crafted and guided by best practices so as not to defeat the initial purpose.

Increasing access to physical inputs

Access to good-quality inputs can be improved by increasing clustering and subcontracting. Instead of competing with small and informal firms for scarce imported inputs, large firms can subcontract input production to small and micro firms. They can work with them and the government to diffuse technology and quality standards so as to improve the quality of inputs. Clustering is especially important for smaller firms because they stand to benefit relatively more from the economies of scales, the reduction of transport costs, the pooling of labor, and the spillovers of technology that are enabled and promoted by clusters. Yamasaki (1996) describes the positive impact of clustering on the dynamism of Japanese small and medium enterprises. Clustered firms are also more likely to export and to adopt process and product innovation than individual firms. The presence of a public research and standards-testing facility and support from public centers or the regional local government can be important elements in the success of clusters, as seen in Indonesia with the clusters to export wood and rattan furniture. There is also evidence of a significant positive relation for small firms between productivity and a subcontractor status (as a supplier) in Asia (Urata and Kwai 2002). Government coordination between businesses and multinational corporations proved crucial in Malaysia to boost a subcontracting partnership to support local small and medium enterprises.

Increasing access to equipment and parts

Competition from informal equipment providers (like *chutos* and *chatarras* in transport) poses a serious threat to the development of a competitive and safe market for equipment. As a consequence, consumers have the choice between very high-standard expensive products and service or low-quality informal ones, leaving in the middle an underdeveloped segment of poorly served consumers. The government can regulate the entry of "informal" equipment and parts, while opening further the trade regime to import more standard and up–to-code equipment and parts. This could be done through removing tariffs, import quotas, or nontariff barriers (such as red tape, cumbersome technical standards) to increase the supply of equipment and parts (McKinsey 2002).

Access to equipment and parts would benefit from the development of financial instruments, such as leasing, to improve the provision of finance for new investment. Leasing allows the lender to retain ownership of the property purchased until the borrower finishes paying off what it owes. Hence, if the borrower defaults on payment, repossession of the good is faster, less costly, and less dependent on the laws and cases on creditors' rights. Leasing also guarantees the creditor that the person will not use the equipment as collateral for other loans. The main challenges for the use of leases are their high administrative costs and insufficient legal guarantees for the borrower.

Increasing access to technology and quality standards

Public technical support increases the diffusion of technological innovation and quality standards to micro and small firms. Innovation is the most important mechanism to increase the production frontier of firms. Technological and scientific progress can be adapted into business innovation by public technology development centers research institutes, trade promotion centers, science parks, and standards laboratories. The government could also foster the development of technology diffusion centers by enabling the industry clusters to promote knowledge spillovers within clusters through cooperation and diffusion. A first step for implementation could be to create economic zones where interaction between suppliers and demand is heightened for specific industries, and suppliers with specialized skills are supported. This could resolve the quality issue of the camelid fiber, facilitate the certification process for wood, and also provide micro and small firms with support on quality standards to step up production and be competitive to access export markets.

Increasing macroeconomic and political stability

Macroeconomic and political stability were at the top of the constraints to functioning for all firms in the 2006 Investment Climate Assessment. Even though the situation has improved in Bolivia since 2006, it is still in the mind of micro and small firms that, as uninsured businesses, they could sustain damages in the event of riots or other disturbances. Those firms also need to be reassured that macroeconomic and political conditions are stable. Such assurances are particularly important when in comes to attracting foreign investment. Thus, macroeconomic and political stability remain necessary but not sufficient conditions for the growth of productivity.

Increasing the profitability of female entrepreneurs

Policy interventions to build capacity among female entrepreneurs include organizing systems to facilitate networking and information-sharing and providing training to build managerial and financial literacy. Carr and Chen (2004) note that while workers in the informal economy were until recently considered unorganized by definition, recent evidence suggests that the informal workforce is being organized by formal trade unions, alternative trade unions, and pro-labor nongovernmental organizations. Common examples are the Self-Employed Women's Association in India (SEWA) and the international alliance of street vendors, StreetNet. Cooperatives are another form through which self-employed women organize and build systems of mutual support and information exchange. Although the potential benefits of training seem obvious, many poor women, especially very small producers and market vendors, are unable to put their acquired skills into practice. Some researchers have suggested that systems of networking and information exchange may often be more valuable interventions than skills and business training alone (Mayoux 1995). Bolivian examples exist, such as the Domestic Workers' Union, and the government should work to strengthen existing and promote new such associations.

Offering childcare services to women entrepreneurs is one way of addressing possible gender-based productivity constraints and provides greater choice to those who choose informality to take care of family. Three quarters of self-employed women say that the ability to care for family members is a very important reason they chose self-employment. Evidence from Colombia (Ribero 2003) and Guatemala (Box 4.4) shows that childcare choices affect not only whether women work, but also the type of work they engage in and the amount of time they spend in paid work.

Box 4.4. Childcare in Guatemala city

Providing childcare for the poor is one way of making occupational segregation by gender more a question of preference than a result of juggling productive and reproductive roles. In poor urban neighborhoods of Guatemala City, finding affordable childcare is a challenge, especially since many poor mothers are migrants who live away from extended family and have less access to informal alternative caregivers.

In Guatemala, the program *Hogares Comunitarios*, a government-sponsored daycare program, supports working parents and, in particular, mothers who are prime income earners. The program was found to benefit two different groups of women:

- *Mothers of participating children.* These are mostly young working mothers, many single. They became more likely to be engaged in formal stable employment, possibly a result of having secured reliable and affordable childcare for extended hours. They also realize higher wages and a larger number of employment benefits than working mothers who use alternative childcare arrangements.
- *Caretakers are mothers themselves.* These are older, less educated women with more limited possibilities to work outside the home. They benefited through the generation of some (albeit low) income.

Although the childcare offered under the program was the cheapest alternative in the areas in which it operated, it was used by only 4 percent of the eligible households. The evaluation states that this outcome was mainly due to limited supply. The program was also found to positively affect food insecurity and malnutrition through cash transfers to caretaker mothers for food.

Source: Hallman et al. 2003.

What Is Bolivia Doing Now to Increase Formalization and Productivity?

The government of Bolivia is already on the right tract to increase formalization and increase productivity. The new National Development Plan, *Plan Nacional de Desarrollo* (PND) is focused on the productive development of micro and small firms (*Micro y Pequenas Empresas*) and on the provision of incentives for firms to formalize. The PND addresses the issue through a three-pronged approach. First, the PND proposes the creation of a second-tier development bank that would improve access to finance for rural producers and urban micro and small firms to increase their capacity and productivity. Second, the PND develops a policy of productive inclusion, which provides incentives to reorganize production through vertical and horizontal integration of productive clusters (*complejos productivos*). Finally, the PND calls for subsidies to help formalize enterprises and promote quality certification. Box 4.5 presents the government's strategy to increase the productivity and formalization of micro and small firms.

The government of Bolivia has made clear efforts to develop the legal framework for reforms, however the implementation has been lagging and the prioritization for action can be improved. For formalization, the ministry of micro and small firms is developing a comprehensive and sector wide approach to formalize all micro and small firms within a limited timeframe. However, the current approach does not distinguish between firms of different size and is heavy on enforcement. Our study suggests that it is necessary to apply different types of policy for different types and sizes of firms as they are differently affected by formality. For productivity, the selection of the productive clusters to receive strategic public investment has been delayed. There is slow progress on the implementation of the legal reforms and on the prioritization of the actions to support the sectoral reforms. A very notable advance is related to the implementation of the National Service for the Productive Development of Small Producers (SENADEPRO). As seen in the study, such services can be instrumental in promoting information about formalization, and providing business support as benefit of formalization.

Box 4.5. Government and private actions on productivity and formality

In June 2006, the government presented the National Development Plan (PND), which includes actions to encourage the productivity and formalization of micro and small firms. The core of this plan proposed to increase the productivity of small and micro enterprise through the creation of a development bank that will finance some productive clusters and through the improvement of government services to support small producers, in particular in the rural areas, supporting the association of micro and small entrepreneurs and their integration, both horizontal and vertical. The development bank was created in January 2007, and the Ministry of Planning, responsible for the implementation of this plan, in coordination with the Ministry of Production and Micro-enterprises, and the Ministry of Rural Development, has selected six clusters—textiles, milk products, wood and furniture, leather and its manufactures, meso-thermal valleys, and Sahapaqui. In this context, the Ministry of Production and Micro enterprises is developing a comprehensive set of policies to encourage greater productivity and coordination between small, medium, and large firms, communities, and associations throughout the six working areas:

(Box continues on next page)

Box4.5 (continued)

- Registry and formalization of small firms in order to increase their productivity and, at the end of the process, collect taxes from them.
- Development of technical and financial services to increase the productivity of small producers mainly through the development bank.
- Creation of a new regulation platform, promotion of free trade zones, and improvement of the quality verification system to promote investment and production quality.
- Opening of domestic and international markets to small producers.
- Diversification of production, both for domestic and export markets, focusing on productive clusters.
- Promotion of new regulation to strengthen productive communities, particularly women.

In line with this strategy, the Ministry of Production and Micro-enterprises has been preparing a comprehensive and sector-wide approach to formalize micro and small firms. The ministry is designing a set of policies to identify and register them, so as to make them better visible and allow them better access to improved government services, including training, access to finance, access to new markets, and linkages to other firms. The strategy considers a temporary tax exemption for three years and the simplification of some registration processes to encourage the massive registration of micro and small firms within a given timeframe. Additionally, the International Labor Organization has proposed a set of policies to increase the registration of firms and workers with the Ministry of Labor, and to improve coordination with the Internal Revenue Service, FundEmpresa, the National Health Institution, and Pension Funds (AFPs).

In this context, the Ministry of Production and Micro-enterprises announced in March 2007 the creation of the National Service for Productive Development (SENADEPRO) together with the reactivation of the Compro Boliviano (I Buy Bolivian) program. The Compro Boliviano program, originally implemented by President Mesa, will deepen the access of micro and small firms, both rural and urban, to massive government procurement processes. To this end, an advisory group will be created, including representatives from producers' organizations. In turn, SENADEPRO will strengthen the technical and managerial capacity of micro and small entrepreneurs to increase their productivity. SENADEPRO, which will begin its operations and financing in July 2007, is already receiving the first candidates. The first sector to be covered is the imported used-clothes commerce: this sector should stop its activities in September 2007. This sector will be supported through training to be provided by SENADEPRO in the production of textiles, jewelry, leather among others, and through Productive Development Bank financing, for up to US$15,000 from a US$5 million fund, with an annual interest rate of 4 percent.

The Ministry of Finance has been pushing for an increase in the supervision of large firms that are registered, as small units, in special tax regimes to evade taxes. In this context, interdepartmental and international transport firms were forced to move from a special tax regime to the general tax regime and hence to pay more taxes in 2006. Actions in other sectors, particularly in wholesale commerce, are being evaluated to improve targeting, in close coordination with Customs and Tax Services agencies. However, these actions are not designed as part of a structured approach to deal with informal firms and are concentrated in only a handful of sectors.

At the subnational level, under the framework of a National Plan for the Simplification of Business Regulation at the Municipal Level, seven Bolivian municipalities have implemented simplification reforms: Santa Cruz, Cochabamba, El Alto, La Paz, Trinidad, Tarija, and Montero. The later four with the support of the IFC. The program has achieved sizable improvements in the number of steps, time consumed and costs of municipal licenses granted, significantly increasing the number of firms registered at this level of government (see Chapter 1). The IFC is planning to extend the reform to five additional municipalities, including the strengthening of local capacities to insure sustainability. Open Workshops on institutional diagnostic will be held in September 2007, to guide municipalities in the identification of operative inefficiencies and in data collection. The active participation of private stakeholders—chambers of commerce and industry, entrepreneurs associations—will be induced.

Although in a more limited scale, the private sector also participated in projects dealing with the informality issue. Additionally to private-managed FundEmpresa, the Cochabamba Chamber of Commerce, with the support of an IADB credit, implemented in 2006 a project to strengthen the managerial skills and to induce formalization of micro and small firms (MyPEs), eventually resulting in their inclusion as members of the Chamber. 600 MSE's belonging to tour sectors—metal works, wood, food and commerce—are participating in the program, which will end in September 2007. The project includes the creation of a permanent office to guide MSE's in the formalization process.

The government proposal to provide subsidized credit to micro and small producers poses risks. The success of the government program will depend on how effective the new development bank can be in increasing intermediation and deepening credit to small and productive firms, while being sustainable and not distorting competition with the current financing system. Indeed, Bolivian microfinance institutions' rates are very competitive and among the best in the region. However, access is low and they are not providing credit to most of the small and micro producers and firms.

The government of Bolivia has built a set of sectoral economic policies (*Plan Sectorial de Desarrollo Productivo*) within the framework of the PND to support the productivity and formality objectives. These goals are also supported by operational and institutional reforms, as well as by providing incentives through easing business registration and licensing, adequate taxation, markets development, incentives to exports, providing standardization and quality control of products (Table 4.1). The government has also identified the need to strengthen productive infrastructure (roads, telecommunications, and energy) as a key element to foster production and improve competitiveness. However, despite the existence of many laws, the implementation is lagging.

Table 4.1. Bolivia's current strategy to increase formality and productivity

Policy recommendations	Government's *Plan Sectorial de Desarrollo Productivo*	
	Policy goal	*Form of implementation*
Improve access to finance.	• Promote access to finance to productive sectors with new financial instruments.	• Law of simplification of processes in the financial sector (*Leyes de Desburocratización del Sistema Financiero*). • Law of movable assets (*Ley de Garantías Bienes Muebles*). • Regulation of the registry of movable assets. (*Reglamento del Registro de Bienes Muebles*). • Law on corporate rule (*Ley de Gobiernos Corporativos*). • Law on financial leasing (*Ley de Leasing Financiero*).
Improve access to inputs.	• Reduce asymmetries in equipment and input for production.	
Improve access to skilled workers and less rigid labor regulations (especially nonlabor costs).	• Training and technical assistance from government.	• The decree on the implementation of the national service for the productive development of small producers (*D.S. de implementación del Servicio Nacional de Desarrollo Productivo del Pequeño Productor* (SENADEPRO)).

(Table continues on next page)

Table 4.1 (continued)

Policy recommendations	Government's *Plan Sectorial de Desarrollo Productivo*	
	Policy goal	*Form of implementation*
Promote domestic and external demand for Bolivian products (trade and customs regulations), as well as standardization and quality control in production.	• Exports diversification (products and markets). • Development of domestic market through government purchases (*Compro Boliviano*). • Standardization and certification. • Increase in production added value. • Fiscal, financial, and institutional incentives to exports. • Protective tariffs. • Smuggling enforcement.	• Training and equipment to the Weather Forecast Institute (*Instituto Boliviano de Metrología* (IBMETRO)). • The law on the promotion of traditional fairs (*Legislación de Reconocimiento de Ferias Ancestrales*). • The law to enter government contracts (*Ley Compro Boliviano*). • The decree of commercial protection (*D.S. Defensa Comercial (Salvaguardias, Dumping y Subvenciones)*). • The decree on unfair international commercial practices (*D.S. Normativa sobre Practicas Desleales de Comercio Internacional*).
Diffusion of technology (training) and promotion of economies of scales by association (clustering and subcontracting).	• Financing research and development. • Association and development of productive sectors (*complejos productivos*). • Economic incentives for strategic alliances and production networks.	• The decree of registration of the different associations of small producers (*D.S. de Registro de Confederaciones, federaciones, cámaras que organizan agrupaciones de los pequeños productores*).
Ease the business licensing and permits registration (lower renewal costs).	• Reduction in bureaucracy and simplification of registration. • Promotion of productive investment.	• The fundamental law of small producers (*Ley Fundamental del Pequeño Productor*). • The decree to formalize and recognize small producers (*D.S. de formalización y reconocimiento del pequeño productor*).
Ease the tax administration and tax rates.	• Promote formalization and adequate taxation for small urban and rural firms.	
Support infrastructure, access to telecommunications, and access to electricity.	• Strengthen productive infrastructure.	

References

AGEXPRONT (*Asociación Gremial de Exportadores de Productos No Tradicionales*). 2005. "Plan de 150 días para la Reactivación del Sector Agrícola No Tradicional en las Áreas Afectadas por la Tormenta Stan."

Alec, R., and Maloney, F. 1998. *The Informal Sector, Firm Dynamics, and Institutional Participation.* Policy Research Working Paper No. 1988, September 1998.

Almeida, R. 2005. *Enforcement of Labor Regulation, Informal Labor, and Firm Performance.* Policy Research Working Paper No. 3756, October 2005.

Balassa, B. 1964. "The Purchasing Power Parity Doctrine: A Reappraisal." *Journal of Political Economy* 72: 584-596.

Borda, D., and J. Ramírez. 2006. *Bolivia: Situación y Perspectivas de las MiPyMEs y su Contribución a la Economía.* Banco Interamericano de Desarrollo. June 2006.

Bruhn, Miriam. 2006. "License to sell: the effect of business registration reform on entrepreneurial activity in Mexico." Mimeo Cambridge, Mass.: MIT.

Canavire, J., and F Landa. 2006. *Duración del Desempleo en el Area Urbana de Bolivia: Un Análisis de los Efectos de Niveles de Instrucción y Características Socioeconómicas.* Revista Análisis Económico – UDAPE. La Paz, Bolivia. 2006.

Carr, M., and M. Chen. 2004. "Globalization, Social Exclusion and Gender." *International Labor Review* 143(1-2).

CEPROBOL, 2005 "ABC del Exportador," a publication from the Vice ministerio de Relaciones Economicas y Comercio Exterior and El Centro de Promocion Bolivia.

Chen, M. 2001. "Women in the Informal Sector: A Global Picture the Global Movement." *SAIS Review* 21(1).

Chen, M. 2005a. *Rethinking the Informal Economy: Linkages with the Formal Economy and the Formal Regulatory Environment.* Research Paper No. 2005/10. Harvard University. WIDER. April, 2005.

———. 2005b. *The Business Environment and the Informal Economy: Creating Conditions for Poverty Reduction.* Harvard University. WIEGO. October, 2005.

Coco, G. 2000. "On the use of Collateral". *Journal of Economic Surveys* 14 (2): 191-214.

Coelho, I., Gñomez, J., Medas, P., and Serra, P. 2004. *Hacia un Sistema Tributario más Eficiente y Justo.* International Monetary Fund.

Cunningham, W. 2001. "Breadwinner of Caregiver? How household Role Affects Labor Choices in Mexico," Washington DC: World Bank.

Cunningham, W. and C. Ramos Gomez, 2002. "The Home as Factory Floor: Employment and Remuneration of Home-based Workers," Washington DC: World Bank.

De Mel, Suresh, David McKenzie, and Christopher Woodruff. 2007. "Returns to Capital in Micro enterprises: Evidence from a Field Experiment." World Bank Policy Research Working Paper. Washington, D.C.

De Soto, H. 1989. *The Other Path: The Invisible Revolution in the Third World*. Harper & Row, New York, 1989.

DFID. 2006. *MyPEs Exportadoras: Consultas sobre Microempresas en Bolivia*. La Paz, Bolivia. July 2006.

DFID-DECMA. 2006. "La Bolivia Invisible, Como Hacerla Visible?" Insertando la Economia Formal.

DFID-DECMA. 2007. "La Bolivia Invisible, Como Hacerla Visible."

Diaz, C., and Rojas, H. 2005. *La Informalidad en Bolivia: Una Válvula de Escape o un Freno para la Economía?* Fundación para la Producción. La Paz, Bolivia. September, 2005.

Encuestas y Estudios. 2007. *Informalidad y Productividad*. Mimeo.

Fajnzylber, Pablo, William Maloney, and Gabriel Montes Rojas. 2006a. "Releasing Constraints to Growth or Pushing on a String? The Impact of Credit, Training, Business Associations and Taxes on the Performance of Mexican Micro-Firms." World Bank Policy Research Working Paper No. 3807. Washington, D.C.

————. 2006b. "Does Formality Improve Micro-Firm Performance? Quasi-Experimental Evidence from the Brazilian SIMPLES program." World Bank Policy Research Working Paper . Washington, D.C.

Farrell, Diana. -2004. "The hidden dangers of the informal economy." *The McKinsey Quarterly* (Number 3). http://www.mckinseyquarterly.com/article_page.aspx?ar=1448&L2=7& L3=10&srid=6&gp=1.

Fundación para el Desarrollo Empresarial, Capacitación y Medio Ambiente (DECMA). 2006. *La Bolivia Invisible. ¿Como hacerla visible? Insertando la economía informal*. La Paz, Bolivia. September 2006.

Galindo, A. and Micco, A. 2004. "Bank Credit to Small and Medium Enterprises: the role of Creditor Protection". Mimeo IADB, Washington DC.

Gasparini, L., and Tornarolli, L. 2007. *Labor Informality in Latin America and the Caribbean: Patterns and Trends from Household Survey Microdata*. Centro de Estudios Distributivos, Laborales y Sociales. Universidad Nacional de La Plata.

Gibson, John, and David McKenzie. 2007. "Using the Global Positioning System (GPS) in Household Surveys for Better Economics and Better Policy." World Bank Policy Research Working Paper No. 4195. Washington, D.C.

Giugale, M. and El-Diwany, S. 1997. *Informality, Size and Regulation. Theory and an Application to Egypt*. Center for Agricultural and Rural Development. Iowa State University. December 1997.

Henley, A., Reza, G., and Carneiro, F. 2006. *On Defining and Measuring the Informal Sector*. World Bank Policy Research Working Paper No. 3866, March 2006.

Hallman, K., A. R. Quisumbing, M. T.Ruel, and B. de la Briere. 2003. "Childcare and Work: Joint Decisions among Women in Poor Neighborhoods in Guatemala City." Washington, D.C.: International Food Policy Research Institute.

IDB. 2005. "Unlocking Credit." In *Economic and Social Progress in Latin America 2005*.Wshington, D.C.: Inter-American Development Bank.

Inter-American Development Bank. 2003. *Good Jobs Wanted: Labor Markets in Latin America. 2004 Economic and Social Progress Report.* Baltimore: The Johns Hopkins University Press.

Instituto Libertad y Democracia (ILD). 2007. *Evaluación Preliminar de la Economía Extralegal en 12 países de Latinoamérica y el Caribe. Reporte de la Investigación en Bolivia. Resumen Ejecutivo.* Lima, Peru.

Instituto Nacional de Estadística (INE). 2006. "Actualidad Estadísticas y Notas de Prensa 2005." www.ine.gov.bo.

International Finance Corporation (IFC). 2007. *Municipal Scorecard 2007. Midiendo las Barreras Burocráticas a Nivel Municipal. Reporte Bolivia.* Washington.

Iqbal, F., and Urata, S. 2002. "Small Business Dynamism in East Asia: An Introductory Overview." *Small Business Economics* 18 (1-12).

Jemio, L. 1999. *Reformas, Crecimiento, Progreso Tecnológico y Empleo en Bolivia.* Serie Reformas Económicas No. 33.

Jiménez, E. and Jiménez, W. 2001 ? *Movilidad Ocupacional y Desempleo en el Area Urbana de Bolivia.* Revista Análisis Económico – UDAPE. La Paz, Bolivia. 2001?

Kaplan, David, Eduardo Piedra, and Enrique Seira. 2006. "Are Burdensome Registration Procedures an Important Barrier on Firm Creation? Evidence from Mexico." Mimeo. Washington, D.C.: World Bank.

Karlan, D. and M. Valdivia, 2006. "Teaching Entrepreneurship: Impact of Business Training on Microfinance Clients and Institutions," Yale University Innovations for Poverty Action, and Jameel Poverty Action Lab.

Katayama, Hajime, Shihua Lu, and James Tybout. 2006. "Firm-level productivity studies: Illusions and a Solution." Mimeo. State College, Pa.: Department of Economics, Pennsylvania State University.

Kaufmann, D., Kraay, A., and Mastruzzi, M. 2006. *Governance Matters V: Governance Indicators for 1996–2005.* The International Bank for Reconstruction and Development, Washington, D.C. September 2006.

Keen, M., Liam, E., Bodin, J., and Summers, V. 2001. *The Modern VAT.* International Monetary Fund, Washington, D.C.

Kikeri, S., Kenyon ,T., and Palmade, Vincent. 2006. "Reforming the Investment Climate: Lessons for Practitioners." *Policy Research Paper* 3986. Washington, D.C.: World Bank.

KPMG. 2004. *KPMG's Corporate Tax Rates Survey.* www.us.kpmg.com/microsite/Global_Tax/CTR_Survey/2004CTRS.pdf. January 2004.

Kumar, A. and Francisco, M. 2005. "Enterprise size, financing patterns, and credit constraints in Brazil". World Bank Working Paper No 49.

Landa, F., Yañez, P, and Arias, O. 2007. *Movilidad Laboral e Ingresos en el Sector Formal e Informal de Bolivia.* Unidad de Análisis de Políticas Sociales y Económicas. La Paz, Bolivia: March 2006. Mimeo.

Larrazabal Córdova, Hernando, 1997. "La Microempresa ante los Desafíos del Desarrollo". La Paz *CEDLA*, Noviembre 1997. 38 p.

Lay, J. 2003. *Informality and Segmentation in the Bolivian Labor Market: Empirical Evidence and Policy Implications.* Instituto de Investigaciones Socio-Económicas. Universidad Católica Boliviana.

Levenson, A., and Maloney, W. 1998. "The Informal Sector, Firms Dynamics, and Institutional Participation." Policy Research Working Paper WPS 1988. Washington, D.C.: World Bank.

Lewis, W. 2004. *The Power of Productivity. Wealth, Poverty and the Threat to Global Stability.* McKinsey & Company, Inc. United States, Chicago: The University of Chicago Press. April 2004.

Loayza, N. 1996. *The Economics of the Informal Sector: A Simple Model and some Empirical Evidence from Latin America.* Carnegie-Rochester Conference Series on Public Policy No. 45 (1996). North-Holland.

Loayza, N. 2004. "The Impact on Growth and Informality: Cross Country Evidence." Policy Research Working Paper WPS3623. Washington, D.C.: World Bank.

———. 1997. "The Economics of the Informal Sector: A Simple Model and Some Empirical Evidence from Latin America." Policy Research Working Paper WPS 1727. Washington, D.C.: World Bank.

Loayza, N., Oviedo, A., and Servén, L. 2005. *The Impact of Regulation on Growth and Informality. Cross-country Evidence.* World Bank Research Working Paper No. 3623. May 2005.

Loayza, N., and Rigolini, J. 2006. *Informality Trends and Cycles.* Policy Research Working Paper No. 4078. December 2006.

Lucas, R. 1978. "On the size distribution of Business Firms." *Bell Journal of Economics,* Autumn, 508-523.

Maloney, W. 2003. *Informality Revisited.* World Bank Policy Research Working Paper No. 2965. January 2006.

Maloney, W. 2006. "Deconstructing Informality: What Makes Informality such a Bad Word." Mimeo. World Bank.

———. 2004. "Informality Revisited." *World Development* WD1536. Washington, D.C.: World Bank.

Mayoux, L., 1995. "From Vicious to Virtuous Circles: Gender and Micro-Enterprise Development." Occasional Paper. New York: United Nations Development Program

———. 2006. *Why Is It So Hard to Talk about Informality? Some Tentative Conjectures.* Chief Economist Office, Latin America and Caribbean, World Bank. Private Sector Development Forum. April 2006.

Mercado, A. and Ríos, F. 2005. *La Informalidad: ¿Estrategia de Sobrevivencia o Forma de Vida Alternativa?* Instituto de Investigaciones Socio-Económicas. Universidad Católica Boliviana. La Paz, Bolivia. April 2005.

Mercado, A. and Ríos, F. 2005. *Elasticidad Cruzada de la Oferta de Trabajo.* Instituto de Investigaciones Socio-Económicas. Universidad Católica Boliviana. La Paz, Bolivia. July 2005.

McKenzie, David, and Christopher Woodruff. 2006a. "A close look at owners of micro enterprises in the retail trade sector in León, Mexico." Mimeo. Washington, D.C.: World Bank.

McKenzie, David, and Christopher Woodruff. 2006b. "Do entry costs provide an empirical basis for poverty traps? Evidence from Mexican micro enterprises" *Economic Development and Cultural Change* 55(1): 3-42

McKinsey. 2002. "Findings, methodology and lessons learned from the work of the McKinsey Global Institute." Report MGI.

Ministerio de la Producción y Microempresa. 2006. "Plan de Desarrollo Productivo con Soberania para vivir Bien."

Ministry of Labor, OIT-FORSAT. 2006. *Bolivia. Registro de Empresas y de Planillas.* Unidad de Análisis de Políticas Sociales y Económicas. FORSAT Project. October–December 2006.

Mønsted, T. 2000. *Wage Differentials between the Formal and the Informal Sector in Urban Bolivia.* Instituto de Investigaciones Socio-Económicas. Universidad Católica Boliviana. La Paz, Bolivia. February 2000.

Monteiro, J., and Asuncao, J. 2006. "Outgoing the Shadows: estimating the impact of bureaucracy simplification and tax cut on formality and investment." Mimeo. PUC Rio.

Monterrey, J. 2003. *El Sector Informal Urbano en Bolivia.* Mimeo. Instituto Nacional de Estadística. La Paz, Bolivia. 2003.

Mosley, P. 1999. "Microfinance and poverty: Bolivia case study." Mimeo. University of Reading. Reading. May 1999.

Nugent and Yhee, 2002. South Korea's SMEs: Achievements, Problems and Policy Issues of Relevance to Developing Countries." In *Small Business Dynamism in East Asia,* Kluwer Academic Publishers.

Paula, A., and Scheinkman, J. 2006. "The Informal Sector." Working Paper. Princeton, N.J.: Princeton University.

Poveda, P. 2003. *Trabajo, Informalidad y Acumulación. Formas de Producción y Transferencia de Excedentes de la Industria Manufacturera Boliviana.* Centro de Estudios para el Desarrollo Laboral y Agrario (CEDLA). La Paz, Bolivia. August 2003.

Pradhan, M., and Soest, A. 1995. *Formal and Informal Sector Employment in Urban Areas of Bolivia.* Labor Economics 2-1995.

Ribero, R. 2003. "Gender Dimensions of Non-formal Employment in Colombia." Documento CEDE, background paper for the Policy Research Report on Gender and Development. Washington, D.C.: World Bank.

Roenhard, T. 2006. *Informality. A Literature Review.* Mimeo.

Rojas, B. and Guaygua, G. 2002. *El Empleo en Tiempos de Crisis.* Centro de Estudios para el Desarrollo Laboral y Agrario (CEDLA). 2002.

Rossell, P. and Poveda, P. 2002. *Reestructuración Capitalista y Formas de Producción.* Centro de Estudios para el Desarrollo Laboral y Agrario (CEDLA). La Paz, Bolivia.

Schneider, F. 2002. *Size and Measurement of the Informal Economy in 110 Countries around the World.* July 2002. Mimeo.

———. 2004. *The Size of the Shadow Economies of 145 Countries all over the World: First Results over the Period 1999 to 2003.* Discussion Paper Series. Forschungsinstitut zur Zukunft der Arbeit. Institute for the Study of Labor. Discussion Paper No. 1431. December 2004.

Schneider, F., and Enste, D. 2000. *Shadow Economies around the World: Size, Causes and Consequences.* International Monetary Fund. Working Paper 00/26. March 2000.

Tannuri.-Pianto, M., and Pianto, D. 2003. *Formal, Informal and Self-employed earnings in Urban Bolivia: Accounting for Sample Selection with Multiple-Choice Models.* July 2003.

Tannuri-Pianto, M., Pianto, D., and Arias, O. 2004. *Informal Employment in Bolivia: A Lost Proposition?* Mimeo.

Unidad de Análisis de Políticas Sociales y Económicas (UDAPE), 2003. "Estrategia Boliviana de Reducción de la Pobreza: Informe de Avance y Perspectivas".

———. 2004. "Estrategia Boliviana de Reducción de la Pobreza (EBRP)." Revised.

———. 2005. *Situación del Empleo en Bolivia. 1999-2003 y Proyecciones*. UDAPE. Ayuda Memoria. October 2005.

———. 2006. Dossier de Estadísticas 2006. http://www.udape.gov.bo/dossierweb2006/htms/dossier16.htm.

Unidad de Productividad y Competitividad. 2006. "Bolivia Productiva: Estrategia de Desarollo Productivo a partir de Complejos Productivos."

USAID. 2005. "Removing Barriers to Formalization: The Case for Reform and Emerging Best Practice." Washington, D.C.: U.S. Agency for International Development.

Urata, S., and Kwai, M. 2002. "Trade and Foreign Direct Investment in East Asia." In *Small Business Dynamism in East Asia*, Kluwer Academic Publishers.

Villegas, H. and Núñez, J. 2005. *Discriminación Etnica en Bolivia: Examinando Diferencias Regionales y por Nicho de Calificación*. Instituto de Investigaciones Socio-Económicas. Universidad Católica Boliviana. La Paz, Bolivia. March 2005.

World Bank. 2004. World Development Report. "A Better Investment Climate for Everyone." Washington, D.C.

———. 2005a. Bolivia Poverty Assessment. "Establishing the Basis for Pro-Poor Growth." Washington, D.C.

———. 2005b. Bolivia Country Economic Memorandum. "Policies to Improve Growth and Employment." Washington, D.C.

———. 2005c. *Doing Business 2005*. "Removing Obstacles to Growth". Washington, D.C.

———. 2001. "Bolivia Microeconomic Constraints and Opportunities for Higher Growth." Pilot Investment Climate Assessment. Washington, D.C.

———. 2006b. Bolivia Policy Notes. "Bolivia, Por el Bienestar de Todos." Washington, D.C.

———. 2006c. Bolivia Interim Strategy Note. Washington, D.C.

———. 2007a. *Informality: Exit and Exclusion*. The International Bank for Reconstruction and Development, Washington, D. C.

———. 2007b. Regional Flagship on Informality 2007. Washington, D.C.: World Bank.

World Bank and International Finance Corporation. 2006. *Doing Business 2007. How to Reform*. The International Bank for Reconstruction and Development, Washington, D. C.

World Economic Forum. 2005. *The Global Competitiveness Report 2005-2006. Creating and Improving Business Environment*. World Economic Forum. Geneva, Switzerland 2005.

———. 2006. *The Global Competitiveness Report 2006-2007. Creating and Improving Business Environment*. World Economic Forum. Geneva, Switzerland 2006.

Yamasaki 2002. "The Evolution and Structure of Industrial Clusters in Japan." In *Small Business Dynamism in East Asia*, Kluwer Academic Publishers.

Yañez, P., and Landa, F. 2007. *Informe Especial. Informalidad en el Mercado Laboral*. Documento de trabajo 01/2007. Unidad de Análisis de Políticas Sociales y Económicas. March 2007.

Eco-Audit

Environmental Benefits Statement

The World Bank is committed to preserving Endangered Forests and natural resources. We print World Bank Working Papers and Country Studies on postconsumer recycled paper, processed chlorine free. The World Bank has formally agreed to follow the recommended standards for paper usage set by Green Press Initiative—a nonprofit program supporting publishers in using fiber that is not sourced from Endangered Forests. For more information, visit www.greenpressinitiative.org.

In 2008, the printing of these books on recycled paper saved the following:

Trees*	Solid Waste	Water	Net Greenhouse Gases	Total Energy
355	16,663	129,550	31,256	247 mil.
*40 feet in height and 6–8 inches in diameter	Pounds	Gallons	Pounds CO_2 Equivalent	BTUs

green press
INITIATIVE

www.ingramcontent.com/pod-product-compliance
Lightning Source LLC
Chambersburg PA
CBHW081507200326
41518CB00015B/2414